RICHARD
PRATT

T0339191

RICHARD

One Out of the Box

PRATT

The Secrets of an Australian Billionaire

James Kirby

Rod Myer

WILEY

John Wiley & Sons Australia, Ltd

First published 2009 by
John Wiley & Sons Australia, Ltd
42 McDougall Street, Milton Qld 4064

Office also in Melbourne

Typeset in Bembo 12.4/15.9 pt

© James Kirby and Rod Myer 2010

The moral rights of the authors have been asserted

Some material in this publication originally appeared in *Richard Pratt: Business Secrets of the Billionaire Behind Australia's Richest Private Company*, published 2004 by John Wiley & Sons Australia

National Library of Australia Cataloguing-in-Publication entry:

Author:	Kirby, James.
Title:	Richard Pratt: one out of the box—the secrets of an Australian billionaire / James Kirby, Rod Myer.
ISBN:	9781742169606 (pbk.)
Notes:	Includes index.
Subjects:	Pratt, Richard, 1934–2009. Visy Paper. Businessmen—Australia—Biography. Philanthropists—Australia—Biography. Billionaires—Australia—Biography.
Other Authors/Contributors:	Myer, Rod.
Dewey Number:	338.43676092

Extract from The World Today 'Richard Pratt warns of coming chronic shortage of water' by Jo Mazzochi, first published by ABC Online, 14 March 2003, is reproduced by permission of the Australian Broadcasting Corporation and ABC Online. © 2003 ABC. All rights reserved.

Cover design by Xou Creative

Cover photo © Fairfax Photo library / Craig Sillitoe

Printed in Australia by McPherson's Printing Group

10 9 8 7 6 5 4 3 2 1

Disclaimer

Contents

About the authors

James Kirby

James is Managing Editor at Australian Independent Business Media, the publisher of online investment magazine Eureka Report and the online business news website Business Spectator. He is also a weekly columnist for *The Sunday Age* and a regular commentator on Sky Business.

He has worked for *The Australian Financial Review*, *The Australian*, *Business Review Weekly*, *Business and Finance* (Dublin) and *The South China Morning Post* (Hong Kong). He is a graduate of University College Galway and of the National Institute of Higher Education (now Dublin City University) in Ireland.

Rod Myer

Rod Myer was born on a farm in north-eastern Victoria and has lived most of his life in Melbourne. He is a writer, journalist and poet with twenty-five years' experience in the Australian media. He has worked as a business writer for *The Age*, *The Sunday Age*, *The Herald* and the *Herald Sun*, and has made radio documentaries for the ABC, 3RRR and Public Radio News. Rod also worked in politics, serving as a speechwriter, political adviser and researcher for the Australian Democrats in the 1980s.

He is the author of *Living the Dream: The Story of Victor Smorgon*, which chronicles the life of the patriarch of the Smorgon industrial dynasty, and has published a work of his own poetry called *Prayers for a Modern Man*.

Prior to commencing a career in writing and journalism Rod spent a number of years living in the outback working in the mining and pastoral industries, and has travelled extensively in Asia, North America and Europe.

Acknowledgements

James Kirby

Thanks again to the team at John Wiley & Sons who have guided me through a variety of challenges since we began working together in 2002. Thanks also to my book editor, Brendan Atkins at Big Box Publishing, for editing the original manuscript and suggesting many improvements along the way.

For the original manuscript Richard Pratt allowed me remarkable access and I remain grateful for the patience he showed at that time in the face of many questions he had no doubt heard before, and some that were clearly being considered for the first time.

Tony Gray, press officer at the Visy group, stands out as the person who did more than anyone else to make the original book a reality.

I would also like to thank a range of people I dealt with when researching the original book, including Gideon Haigh, Robbie Kaye, Sam Lipski, Bill Montague, Anthony Pratt, Michael O'Regan and Adrian Tame.

Finally, thanks once more to my partner, Mary O'Brien, who shared thoughts, theories and reflections on the original book as it came together.

Rod Myer

Writing this book would not have been possible without the support and assistance of a number of people. I would particularly like to thank my co-author James Kirby, Tony Gray, Michael Naphtali, Rebecca Myer, Ian Allen, Digger James, Sam Lipski, Leon Zwier, Helen Reisner, Stephen Kernahan, Keith McKenzie, Paul Littmann, Julia Fraser, Dr George Klempfner, Brian Meltzer and Winsome McCaughey.

I have also cited the published work of a number of journalists whose diligence and talent I am grateful for. Most prominent among these are Garry Linnell, Leonie Wood, Cameron Stewart, Annette Sharp, Patrick Smith and Jake Niall.

I would also like to thank the publisher, John Wiley & Sons Australia, particularly my editors Kristen Hammond and Kate Romaniotis.

Introduction

The last days of a king

In mid April 2009 a seemingly endless stream of visitors began making their way to Raheen, the mansion belonging to Richard and Jeanne Pratt in the leafy Melbourne suburb of Kew. Richard Pratt had been diagnosed with prostate cancer in 2006, but he was not the sort of person to lie down and go quietly. He was a fighter and a visionary who was accustomed to shaping life according to his whim. So he fought—so strongly that he once appeared at an informal business meeting with an intravenous needle still in his arm. He had apparently considered his treatment finished for the day and, unable to catch the attention of the hospital staff and unwilling to miss his meeting, he simply pulled the tube delivering his medication out of the needle and walked out.

The disease eventually went into remission, only to reappear in 2009. What appeared at first to be an abscess on his prostate was in fact cancer. In March he was in severe pain, which forced him to be often, and uncharacteristically, away from the office. Then one weekend in early April his condition deteriorated and he was taken to hospital. There he was told that the disease had spread to his lungs and liver, and that his life was coming to an end.

The family let it be known that Richard Pratt's days were numbered, and so began the succession of people—a mixture of the rich, the powerful, the well known and the unknown— to Raheen to pay their last respects to a man who had touched myriad lives across the community. Former Labor opposition leader and current Trade Minister Simon Crean joined the throng, as did the former skipper of Australia's successful 1983 America's Cup challenge John Bertrand. Various Carlton Football Club personalities, including legend Ron Barassi, president and former skipper Stephen Kernahan, coach Brett Ratten, captain Chris Judd and club Chief Executive Greg Swann, said their goodbyes. Former long-term employees of Visy, Pratt's giant packaging company, such as Cliff Powell, with whom the ailing tycoon sang a duet as they had done often over the previous fifty years, and Dante Bastiani, came to see their old boss one last time. Socialite Lillian Frank also made the journey, saying later that the Pratts were like family to her.

Outspoken and unconventional ally of the downtrodden Father Bob McGuire and trucking magnate Lindsay Fox joined the queue. Pratt's long-time mistress Shari-Lea Hitchcock was allowed to spend one hour with the man she loved and had a daughter with. Prime Minister Kevin Rudd also made an unscheduled fifteen-minute visit to the bedside of the dying billionaire.

On the day before his death it was announced that evidence used to charge Richard with four counts of giving false and misleading evidence to an inquiry into price-fixing allegations by the Australian Competition and Consumer Commission had been ruled inadmissible and all charges had been dropped. Upon receiving word of the ruling, Pratt's daughter Fiona leaned across her father, who was drifting in and out of consciousness, and whispered the news in his ear. Pratt reportedly nodded signalling he understood and began to weep.

The Cardboard King passed away on 28 April 2009 with his family by his side. Following Pratt's death a range of public figures, including the Prime Minister, expressed regret at his passing and thanks for the contributions he made in a range of areas. Even his adversary in the final months of his life ACCC Chairman Graeme Samuel expressed his sadness.

Two days after his death a section of Kew was closed off by police as 500 people crammed into the suburb's synagogue, while another 500 stood outside watching closed circuit television coverage of Pratt's funeral. Once again there was a wide cross-section of the community present, from friends and relatives to businesspeople, sportspeople, politicians and even the centurion philanthropist and mother of media magnate Rupert, Dame Elisabeth Murdoch. In his eulogy to his long-time friend, Pratt Foundation Chief Executive Sam Lipski observed that he knew of no other Australian whose life and death had touched so many people.

Richard Pratt, the migrant boy from Poland who set out from his parents' fruit block in the country town of Shepparton in

Victoria, built far more than the Visy packaging empire that catapulted him to the status of richest man in Australia. He influenced people, organisations, public policy and culture across an unusually broad spectrum using not only his money, but his ideas, passion and boundless energy. His was a remarkable journey.

Chapter 1

From Poland to Shepparton and beyond

Richard Pratt (born Ryszard Przecicki) was born in what was then known as the Free City of Danzig on the Baltic coast of Poland in December 1934 to Jewish parents Leon and Paula Przecicki. Events in Danzig were something of a precursor to the storm that would rain down on Europe in the late 1930s. Although firmly part of Poland, situated on the mouth of the Vistula River that runs through Warsaw, it also has strong links with Germany. During the Middle Ages it was a member of the Hanseatic League of predominately German cities that dominated trade in the Baltic. In the centuries that followed its administration moved between the Germanic state of Prussia and the Polish kings. Prior to World War I it had been part of Imperial Germany and following the recreation of Poland after 1918 it took on the status of a 'free city', a small, almost independent state in its own right.

Danzig was not given to the new Polish state in 1918 because around ninety-eight per cent of its inhabitants were German. As Hitler rose to power he demanded the return of Danzig to German control and he sent his henchmen to watch the city's Jewish community in what was an early sign of the bleak future for European Jewry under Nazi domination. From the mid 1930s the Jewish population, wisely as it turned out, started to leave Danzig for Britiain and other parts of Europe. World War II actually began in the city when the German battleship *Schleswig-Holstein* bombarded Polish positions at Westerplatte.

Post–World War II the city was fully integrated into communist Poland and went by its Polish name, Gdansk. It was famed for the rise of the Solidarity trade union at its Lenin Shipyards in 1980 under the leadership of Lech Walesa. The movement was the first independent union in Eastern Europe since before the days of Soviet domination. Its activism proved so successful that years of martial law could not crush it and by 1989 it was the main opposition to the Polish communist government. Elections that year saw a Solidarity-led government and in December 1990 the shipyard electrician Walesa was elected Polish president.

Danzig was a vibrant place with a traditionally open culture, and the Pratt family were loath to leave it. For years Leon Pratt ignored the darkening clouds of Nazism and clung to life with his bike shop in the port city. Eventually, he could no longer ignore the danger and in 1938 made his way to London. He left Paula with enough money to follow him later when he sent for her. However, some months on when he sent word for her and young Richard to come there were major problems. The outflow of Jewish refugees as the situation in Europe worsened meant host countries were shying away from accepting people. Paula approached a number of consulates but could not find one that would give her and three-year-old Richard a visa. In the end the Swedish consulate obliged and, with the help of a kindly stranger at the port of Danzig, she found berth on a ship that took them to London. Later Richard would say he had 'escaped the Holocaust by about five minutes'.

The years of Poland's Nazi occupation would wash away the world Richard Pratt was born into. Pre-war, Poland was the centre of Jewish culture and traditional learning, and Polish Jewry's 3.5 million people made up ten per cent of the nation's population. Between 1939 and 1945 ninety per cent of them were killed and most of the rest fled, leaving only a few thousand Jews in Poland at the war's end. The religious scholars in their *yeshivot* (study houses), the writers and performers, the Yiddish theatres, and the traders and industrialists who had created so much of the material and spiritual wealth of Poland were gone, never to return.

Richard Pratt would eventually return to Poland as an adult, though he clearly, like many Polish Jewish émigrés to Australia, had mixed emotions about his birthplace. As a leading international business figure, he was offered Polish citizenship, which he declined.

In London the Pratts discovered that Australia—through the offices of the then federal interior minister John 'Black Jack' McEwen—was allowing Jewish refugees to enter the country. Sailing on a liner called the *Orontes* the young family arrived in Melbourne with 2000 pounds and looked for a way to make a living. They found accommodation in a rooming house in St Kilda, but try as he might Leon could not find a suitable job. He was advised that there was a small Jewish community in the Goulbourn Valley town of Shepparton, in northern Victoria, that had managed to get a foothold in the fruit business, which sounded like a good opportunity. One day Leon arrived home to tell Paula he had put up their 2000 pounds as a deposit on a sixty-acre fruit block at Shepparton. Despite their predilection for urban life, the Pratts, as they now called themselves, headed for country Victoria.

In Shepparton the Pratts were guided by a successful fruit grower named Moses Feiglin. He helped them settle on the fruit block and asked their new neighbour Tom James to take the family under his wing and show them how to make a living in what to them was a totally alien environment. Tom agreed and the Pratts got a start in their new life. The James and Pratt families lived in identical weatherboard cottages separated by a small irrigation channel, and Richard became very close to the neighbouring family.

Tom James had five sons and Richard became lifelong friends with the youngest, William 'Digger' James. 'Richard was my little brother, my little mate', Digger recalled. 'He picked up English very quickly because he was a kid and going to school, and he became the spokesman for the family.' Richard quickly took to farm life and later would reminisce about his days picking peas, digging irrigation channels and driving produce to town in the family truck at the age of thirteen. Digger remembered hearing young Richard singing in the fields as he went about his work.[1]

The relationship with Digger James was to be a highly significant one. Digger, as his nickname suggests, carved out a distinguished military career reaching the rank of major general, serving as the army's chief medical officer and becoming the national president of the RSL. He served in the Korean War where he tragically lost a leg. Richard was nothing if not loyal to the friend who had introduced him to Australian life, regularly visiting him at the Heidelberg Repatriation Hospital in Melbourne while Digger was recovering from his wounds, and carrying his disabled friend to his car and taking him for a drive.[2] On retiring from the army in 1985 Digger ran a Visy factory in Brisbane, and, at the age of seventy-nine, still works three days a week for Visy.

Farm life did not really agree with the Pratts. They were used to a more cultured existence but stuck with the fruit block until the late 1940s. Leon Pratt was an entrepreneur and started looking for other possibilities to boost the farm income. He came up with making boxes for local growers to pack their produce in. At first he made them from wood but later moved to cardboard. When Richard was sixteen the family hitched its wagon to the box business and moved to Melbourne to set up a box factory in a small shopfront in the then industrial suburb of Fitzroy.

Behind every great business empire there is more than one person or more than one family. In the case of the Visy group, it was not entirely a Pratt family operation in the early days. Richard's uncle, Max Plotka, had joined the family in Shepparton after moving from Europe and was part of the move into box making. Digger James later described him as having been damaged by his war experiences. He bore a concentration camp number tattooed on his arm and did not take to country life, moving to Melbourne and marrying Ida Visbord. Starting out in the box business in Melbourne

Max and Leon met an engineer named Les Feldman, and the Feldman family joined the partnership as well. Together they created what was the beginning of the Visy empire.

In the early days Visy was not what you would call a sophisticated corporate operation. To go into box production the company needed a corrugator—a machine that turns paper into cardboard. As none was available Leon, Max and Les approached two engineers, Bill and Ken Allen, and asked if they could build them one. The Allens' younger brother Leon, who worked for many years at Visy, later recalled, 'My older brother said yes [they could build a corrugator]. We didn't even know what a corrugator was and our factory was only fifteen by twenty feet'. Ken Allen was a practical guy and set to work fulfilling the order. He worked out what a corrugator was and began to design one. 'We used to draw our plans on the floor with a piece of chalk. The only problem was we'd just finish a drawing and someone would come and sweep the floor', Ken later remembered.[3] The Allen brothers built the first machine from scrap metal from Ma Dalley's famous scrap yard in North Melbourne. The rollers were made from old gun barrels. When it was finished Leon Allen left his job at Kodak to set up the machine and oversee the running of it, becoming one of Visy's first non-family employees.

Eventually the Pratts bought out the two partners, but, not surprisingly, there have been tensions between the families over who did what in the early days of Visy. The most public tension has been between the Feldmans and the Pratts. Les Feldman, one of the original directors of Visy, publicly campaigned in the 1990s to detail the family's role in the formative years of the company. Feldman wrote to *BRW* magazine detailing the family's early working life in the corrugated board industry and their relationship with the Pratt and Plotka families. The Feldmans clearly believed they had not been given due recognition for their early role in the development of Visy, with Les Feldman claiming that at the time of Visy's foundation he had more experience in the corrugated board sector than anyone else in the group.

Although the Feldmans left Visy in the late 1950s to go to Israel, the link between the two families was not broken at this time. Indeed, the relationship remained cordial with the Feldmans later selling another company, Cardboard Tubes and Cartons, to the Pratts. Richard was obviously working on improving the relationship between the founding families in 2002, when he introduced the Feldmans into Visy's official history. Visy's Director of Sustainability and long-serving Pratt family confidant Tony Gray says the Feldmans were never excluded from the story, rather, they simply did not make it into the abbreviated versions of the company history that had been published. For the record, company documents from 1950 list six directors: Leon and Paula Pratt, Max and Ida Plotka, and Jack and Leslie Feldman.

The Feldman family has also claimed that the name Visy Board, as the company was originally known, came from a Les Feldman idea that they were working with 'visible boards'. However, the accepted source of the name is Ida Plotka's maiden name, Visbord. Ida had invested 100 pounds in the business in its early days.

Whatever the finer details of the story, it is clear that Visy, in the days when the Feldmans, Plotkas and Pratts were working in association, was little more than another of Melbourne's 'backyard' manufacturing companies that dotted the city until the 1980s. It was under Richard Pratt that the company became a multinational, employing almost 9000 people. The change to Visy's history in its 2002 annual review cost Richard nothing, but clearly gave greater recognition to the Feldman family, giving them a place in the economic history of Australia.

Leon Pratt was an entrepreneur and taught his son everything he knew about business. Richard was a natural salesman and started working in the business in 1952 at the age of eighteen. Leon, from whom Richard inherited drive, discipline and the capacity for hard work typical of many migrants, and his Uncle Max Plotka imbued Richard with a sense of pride in running a successful business. He also gained a large dose of business acumen from his mother, Paula, who was closely involved in the development of Visy in the early days.

Leon taught his son the value of engaging with clients, an approach he would develop into the massive parties Visy still throws today. Leon would often get box buyers together at his Albert Park flat and give them gifts of the gadgetry he loved to collect. It made dealing with the Pratt family popular among the buyers and helped the business grow.

A hard worker, Leon drove his son to produce the results he wanted. Observers from those days report that he did not always approve of Richard's extracurricular activities and wondered out loud at times whether he was the right man to take over the business. Richard was a high-spirited young man who liked a good time. Cliff Powell, a lifelong Visy employee, described the young Richard Pratt as 'the wildest young man I've ever seen'.[4] Other Visy employees from that era worried that as a salesman he drove his FJ Holden so fast he was risking his life. However, like Kerry Packer, another successful businessman who was underestimated by his father, Richard was to take the business to new heights unimaginable when his father ran things.

Richard was an enthusiastic and talented salesman with a gift for understanding what made people tick. He could laugh and schmooze with people, and loved telling stories and jokes. In his early years at Visy he brought in prized new customers such as the Rosella, Kraft, Heinz and Tom Piper food labels. He did not pay great attention to detail, though, and tended to promise customers delivery times that were too quick for the factory to meet, which caused some friction between father and son.

After the family moved to Melbourne Richard attended University High School, a coeducational selective school that took students with strong academic abilities. He excelled at athletics and football and was made a prefect. Long-time friend and current Chief Executive of The Pratt Foundation, Sam Lipski, was at University High with Pratt but was three years younger. He recalls that the school held religious instruction classes for the different faiths represented in the student body. The first time Lipski attended the Jewish religion class he was surprised to see Pratt walk in. 'My God, Pratt's Jewish', he thought, surprised because Jewish sporting champions were few and far between at that time.

Even at high school Pratt was a natural leader. 'Wherever you looked he was captain of this or had won a school medal for that', recalls Sam. 'He was good at footy, cricket and athletics, he was in the choir and the school play, he was house captain and he became a prefect. He was so exuberant and extroverted. He was strikingly built and had that presence. When Richard came into a room you knew he was there.'

Pratt did two years of matriculation at University High, graduating in 1952. He then moved on to The University of Melbourne to study commerce. Academic life did not agree with him, however, and he left to work in his father's business. Sam Lipski observed of his university days, 'Richard couldn't sit around waiting to finish; it's not in his temperament to wait for things to happen. He wants things to happen now!' Despite his early exit from university, Pratt went on to receive several honorary degrees later in life. These include an Honorary Doctorate in Engineering from Monash University, an Honorary Doctorate for services to education and the community from Swinburne University of Technology, an Honorary Doctor of Laws from Melbourne University, an Honorary Doctoral Degree for business leadership, philanthropy and water research from Israel's Ben Gurion University of the Negev, and an Honorary Doctorate for his support of the institution and Israel from Hebrew University.

While at university Pratt discovered a new love—acting. He took part in university reviews and became part of the Union Theatre Repertory Company, the precursor to the Melbourne Theatre Company, which in those days was based at Melbourne University.

Australian playwright Ray Lawler directed at the Union and was looking for someone to play Hal Carter, a former football star turned drifter, in the William Inge play, *Picnic*. In footballer and burgeoning actor Richard Pratt he found his man. The casting was a success and in 1955 Lawler offered him a part in his own ground-breaking play *Summer of the Seventeenth Doll*. The play, which depicted crumbling relationships and fading idealism in the conformist 1950s, was a huge success and became one of a handful of Australian plays known worldwide.

The role of Johnnie Dowd, leader of a cane-cutting gang, down from Queensland to spend the layoff season drinking and womanising in the city, promised Richard a fast track to a life on stage and screen.

He accepted the part and a successful season in Australia was followed by seasons in London and New York. The play was a hit in London and while in that city Richard met Max Shavitsky, a young Australian doctor who was impressed with Pratt's thespian abilities and acclaim. A full-sized picture of the young actor was, at that stage, hanging in the window of a West End theatre and his social circle included Sir Laurence Olivier. New York audiences were less impressed, unable to understand the Australian accents and the foreignness of the play. However, actor Burt Lancaster, who had an interest in a film production company called Hecht Hill Lancaster, was impressed enough with the muscular young actor with the rich baritone voice to invite Richard to Hollywood for a screen test for the movie *The Unforgiven*, which was released in 1960. Richard did not get the part, but the company did offer him a studio contract that would have tied him to the company for seven years and was considered a 'slave deal' in the industry.

Max Shavitsky had become a friend and confidant to Pratt, and helped him to negotiate his acting career. 'We used to discuss it quite openly', recalls Max. 'There was a certain romanticism involved. But during this time, he kept receiving letters from his father. They would be along the lines of: "We've got a great business here. It's an expanding business. Your position is to come back and work for it. Stop listening to this rubbish about going into acting. You have to make a decision".'[5]

Pratt chose to return to Australia and the family company in early 1958. 'In his heart, his loyalty to his family became the main factor [in his decision to quit acting and return home]', says Shavitsky. 'Loyalty and obligation.'[6] Richard's career as an actor did not come to a complete stop — he made a brief comeback in 1959, playing Moe Axelrod in a production of Clifford Odets' *Awake and Sing* staged by Melbourne Jewish theatre company The Habima Players (Habima is Hebrew for the stage) and directed by Neuman Jubal, a giant of Viennese theatre in the 1930s.

While Pratt liked the stage, performing in about twelve plays during the 1950s, to him the vagaries of the acting life paled next to the possibilities he knew awaited him in the family business back in Melbourne. Ray Lawler says, '[He] had a choice of being an actor or a multimillionaire'; Richard chose the career with a more certain course.[7]

He continued to enjoy a long involvement with the arts, culminating in his years as chair of the Victorian Arts Centre and his support of his wife, Jeanne, as chair of The Production Company. His colourful and diverse early days clearly infused his later life with interests in the wider world that many businesspeople find hard to develop. He found it amusing that management consultants began looking at areas such as the arts or music as models for developing creativity in the workplace. Said Richard in 2004, 'Fifty years ago I was in London working on stage at the West End and going to every play I could afford on my days off. I saw them all — Laurence Olivier and that whole generation of actors. It was a marvellous experience, and it was part of my education'.

The Visy Richard Pratt returned to in 1958 was a very different company from the one he had left three years earlier.

Business was booming as the consumer revolution swept post-war Australia and production had skyrocketed. The old Fitzroy factory had been abandoned for larger premises, first in Preston then in Thornbury, the machinery was running twenty-four hours a day and Leon Allen had been joined by seventy other workers. The Thornbury factory was getting to be too small, so Leon Pratt had purchased a large site in Reservoir and had built a new factory, soon to be the major production facility for the company.

Leon established a culture of learning and self-improvement in the company that continues today. Two workers from those times, George Robertson and Rod Ledgar, were told by Leon that they needed to upgrade their educational qualifications, so they completed three one-year courses. They would show Leon each new certificate and were told, 'I must pay you more money because you know much more'. Pratt senior also invited them and their girlfriends to his home to be wined and dined during what they later described as a very enjoyable evening. This culture of making the staff and main customers feel valued was important to the Pratt family, and the tradition of extravagant Christmas parties that became so famous during Richard's time at the helm actually began under Leon in 1957. He and Paula held a Christmas party at their Kew home for some staff and key clients including Kraft, Tom Piper and Unilever.

There was an awkward moment early in the evening when no-one knew how things were to proceed. Richard, the natural entertainer, was away in New York and there was not even a piano for entertainment. Cliff Powell, at that stage a new employee, took the initiative and decided to sing. He sang 'Some Enchanted Evening' and 'Old Man River', and then with his wife Gwyneth sang 'Paradise for Two'. The idea took off and the following year Richard and Powell teamed up for a duet. For decades the two sang duets at Visy events and Richard Pratt's solo performances at company functions were one of his trademarks.

Giving up acting and returning to Visy marked a turning point for Richard Pratt. He stopped being the wild man of his youth and settled down to business. He had a reputation for being quite a rake, but in 1959 he met a young Sydney journalist named Jeanne Lasker, who had written for *The Daily Telegraph*, then owned by the Packer family, and had a strong reputation in the media. She was born in 1936 in the little Polish town of Lowicz, not far from Gdansk, and came to Australia as a baby with her parents.

The two had quite an effect on each other and within three days of meeting they were engaged. 'He was the best-looking young man you've ever seen, drop-dead gorgeous but also quite shy', Jeanne later remembered.[8] In June 1959 the couple were married and over the next four years had three children. Anthony was born in 1960, Heloise in 1962 and Fiona in 1964. In 1974 Jeanne came out of journalistic retirement to work on the program *No Man's Land*, a half-hour news and current affairs program on Channel Nine, produced and staffed totally by women.

Jeanne's entry to the program was said to have been preceded by a call to presenter and producer Micki de Stoop from Nine owner Kerry Packer asking if she would agree to the move. De Stoop apparently had high regard for Pratt and agreed. Jeanne had ambitions beyond the average run-of-the-mill journalist, telling a colleague at one point that she wanted eventually to buy a television station and working on the show would be good experience. Workmates considered Jeanne to be a diligent journalist, although she was unfamiliar with television journalism when she arrived. She was older than most of the other reporters and was considered generous in sharing her life experience with them. Susan Peacock, then wife of former Liberal leader Andrew Peacock, was also a reporter on the program.

Jeanne suggested the program's weekly staff meeting, generally held at the Bridge Hotel in Richmond near the Nine studios, be held at the Pratt home instead. The young journalists were stunned by the size of the house. At one point Richard appeared to say hello, and someone asked him what he did. He modestly replied that he made cardboard boxes.

No Man's Land was no lightweight show. On one famous occasion one of its reporters, Gail Jarvis, later a television executive, wanted to get an interview with Frank Sinatra during his famous 1974 Australian tour, marketed as 'Old Blue Eyes is Back'. Certain he would not agree to the request Jarvis hired a white Mercedes and a driver and drove to Tullamarine airport dressed as Sinatra's then partner Barbara Marx. The impostors managed to infiltrate the star's motorcade, following his car, and on the freeway began taking pictures of him. Sinatra realised what was happening and drove straight to Festival Hall, where a mix up saw him having to run the gauntlet of female journalists as he entered the building. As a result he made his infamous 'hookers of the press' remarks on stage during an abusive monologue, triggering union bans on his tour.

The farce ended with Sinatra dashing to the airport to get out of town. At Tullamarine a throng of journalists and then ACTU chief Bob Hawke stood on the tarmac expecting a negotiated settlement that would allow Sinatra's plane to depart. But the feisty crooner ordered his plane to leave, disregarding Hawke's command to the control tower that it be blocked. Sinatra took off for Sydney while in Melbourne the newspaper headlines screamed 'Old blue eyes is black'.

⁓⁓

As the 1960s wore on, the founders of Visy moved into ill health. Max Plotka passed away in 1966 and Leon Pratt was stricken with bad asthma, which started to shorten his work days. In 1969 he too passed on, and direction of the company went to Richard. Paula worried about her son's ability to carry out his new responsibilities. There was no doubting Richard's skills as a salesman, but he was only thirty-four, was not a man who liked to keep up with administrative detail and there was doubt in the minds of some as to how much he knew about the company's accounts and financial position. Paula asked a family friend, Leon Lunski, who had played cards with her late husband, to act as a mentor. He was reluctant as he had recently retired after developing and selling a chain of eight cake shops at the age of fifty-five, but eventually agreed to help out for one year.

Visy at that stage was a company turning over $5 million with only one plant at Reservoir and the doomsayers predicted the company was now through. Competitors wanted to buy Visy and some told Richard he was not half the man his father was. However, the concerns some harboured about Richard's abilities were soon put to rest. He may not have been great with detail but he made up for that with drive and determination and was full of ideas, as Leon Lunski was soon to discover.

Lunski had had a tough life. Polish born, he had served in the Polish army during World War II, and survived Russian slave labour camps and prisons in the Arctic Circle. He had lived through the communist takeover of Poland after the war and had made the adjustment to living in Australia. In old age he told Sam Lipski that after his war experiences he thought he would never find anyone who could scare him, but that his first year at Visy was a real challenge. He had, 'survived the Germans and the Russians but had never come across anyone as powerful and strong willed as Richard Pratt', he told Lipski.[9]

The main source of angst for Lunski was that Richard came up with fifty new ideas at every weekly meeting and charged Lunski with implementing them. This, of course, was impossible and the worry stopped him sleeping at night. Eventually he learned that Pratt came up with many ideas but wanted those close to him to simply find which one would work and implement it. Lunksi stayed on after the first year, becoming 'the feared purchasing manager of the company. He'd squeeze till the pips hurt. It didn't matter whether he was buying paper clips or paper machines', Lipski recalled.

Although Richard Pratt was a man of many talents who could have pursued several different careers, he ultimately threw his lot in with the family business. Partly because he realised it was how he could make the most of his talents in terms of financial and personal achievement, and partly out of a sense of duty to carry on what his parents had started, and in doing so build a base of stability and prosperity for future generations of the Pratt family. Visy was to become his life, his love, his obsession and the vehicle that would take him to places he could not have dreamed of as a young man.

Chapter 2

The beginning of an empire

The 1970s dawned with Richard Pratt in control of Visy. The Plotkas and Feldmans were gone and Leon Pratt's business philosophy soon gave way to that of his son. The two men were close and shared much of the decision-making after Max Plotka passed away. Leon's death was a huge shock to his son.

Father and son had agreed on a lot of things but in the last years of Leon's life they had diverged on one key point. Leon thought that Visy should have only one production site, while Richard saw the need for expansion. Richard's view was solidified by the move of Visy's largest customer, the Lever & Kitchen soap and detergent group, to centralise its production in Sydney. The company accounted for ten per cent of Visy's then $5 million output from its Reservoir plant, and servicing it in Sydney meant sending ten semitrailer loads of cartons north each day risking delays and accidents. Then another big customer, soft drinks manufacturer Tarax, also opened a Sydney plant. Richard knew Visy would lose significant business from both customers if nothing was done to accommodate these changes.

Richard responded decisively, buying industrial land at Warwick Farm in Western Sydney. He opened this second factory in 1970 and sent over some key executives to get things going. He also instigated a new communication regime, whereby his executives were in constant contact with him, to ensure the risks he was taking were being managed properly and that any problems could be dealt with quickly.

Initially, working at the Sydney plant was a tough gig with the executives working seven days a week, but the plant was established and functioning by the end of 1970. Some of those who helped to establish it became Visy stalwarts, most notably Kevin Bamford who, after a long career with the Pratts, established his own successful label manufacturing business.

Richard Pratt's style in those days could be described as a mixture of caution and calculated risk-taking. As he expanded the business on the national stage, Richard began differentiating himself from his father. He realised that in order to continue the growth begun by his father in the 1960s Visy's manufacturing footprint had to expand along with Australia's manufacturing industry. After Warwick Farm another plant was built at Noble Park in Melbourne's south-east in 1975 and a separate operation for printing labels was also developed near the Reservoir plant.

Along with the business, Richard Pratt was developing his own leadership style. In the late 1970s his sidekick Leon Lunski described this style as being based on 'communication, communication, communication'. Like his father before him Richard had the ability to attract and inspire good people but also had greater flexibility, an unusual measure of determination and the ability to take calculated risks that grew the business dramatically. He paid a lot of attention to rewarding staff with higher than average salaries, travel perks, gifts such as tickets to the football and his own personal attention. This inspired a great deal of loyalty, and a number of people stayed with the company for decades.[1]

Richard's personality and confidence were still evolving and he was described by observers as being shy, especially with the media, and as looking for consensus in decision-making. Later in life he used the media like a public relations pro, and while he did not look for unnecessary trouble, he used a kind of creative conflict to draw people out and get the most out of business meetings. In later years he also became moody and could at times appear disengaged, but staff came to understand this aspect of his personality and knew that if he was aggressive or disinterested one day, the next day he would once again be talkative and engaged.

As the company grew and as Richard grew into his new role, managing and planning family life was by and large left to Jeanne. However, he participated in the events she planned and had a strong relationship with his children. He did not take long holidays, but would spend a few days with the family away from work when time allowed. He later said he had to give up some of what most people would consider a normal life to achieve his success.

Pratt's vision continued to grow as the 1970s progressed. He expanded the Warwick Farm plant, began to spend on research and development, and built a new box plant at Carole Park in Brisbane. He had a kind of restlessness that meant he was always looking for new business opportunities. He explored investment opportunities across the Tasman but nothing eventuated.

At that point Australian production of brown paper for cardboard box making was dominated by APM (which became Amcor) and Smorgon Consolidated Industries, a private industrial operation owned by the Russian émigré Smorgon family. Smorgon had its origins in a small kosher butcher shop in Lygon Street in Carlton in the late 1920s, but the company had since grown to a gargantuan size.

As the 1970s drew to a close Richard Pratt looked at the industry and saw that much of the packaging margin was being harvested by the paper manufactures and began to toy with the idea of making paper. He travelled to Italy and at the Toschi plant he saw a small paper machine fed by recycled material that had been ordered in a sale that had since fallen through. Pratt bought this and another similar machine, installing the former at his Warwick Farm plant.

This move worried the incumbent papermakers, particularly Smorgon, which wanted to keep its place in the market. The family patriarch, Victor Smorgon, tried to convince APM's new chief Stan Wallis that he should act to somehow squeeze Pratt out of the market, telling him, 'You're mad Stan. Why don't you do something? Dick Pratt's going to start making paper'.[2]

Wallis of course had neither the intent nor the legal means to taking punitive action against Visy, which was a major APM customer at the time. As a result, by 1980 a second paper machine had been installed at Visy's Reservoir plant, and Richard Pratt was in exactly the position Victor Smorgon had feared he would be—firmly ensconced in the paper business, albeit in a very small way.

Although Visy grew dramatically throughout the 1970s, the company was still run on a fairly informal basis. Then in 1978 Richard Pratt hired Michael Naphtali, a young investment banker who had been running the corporate advice division of Hill Samuel, the forerunner of Macquarie bank, in Melbourne. Naphtali, who was in his thirties at the time, took some months to accept Pratt's offer, as he was reluctant to leave the buzzing world of Collins Street and the finance markets for the workaday environment of Visy's Reservoir headquarters in Melbourne's industrial north.

Naphtali stood apart from other Visy employees as he was highly qualified academically. To assuage workmates inclined to distrust those without factory floor experience, Pratt introduced Naphtali as someone working for the Pratt family, rather than for the company itself. His appointment signalled Pratt's acceptance of the need to connect to the world of high finance.

Naphtali's first job was to buy out the family of Josephine Morris, Pratt's younger Australian-born sister who had passed away in 1974. Richard was rocked by her death and wanted to ensure her family were well provided for. Naphtali came up with a generous deal that adequately compensated Josephine's family, and left Richard's immediate family as the sole proprietors of Visy.

Next Naphtali set about developing more formalised financial management at Visy. 'To this day I'm amazed to think that a company that was turning over $50 million a year [ten times the turnover when Richard took control nine years earlier] really had so few control systems', Naphtali has since said.[3] He describes Visy's banking relationship as 'hand-to-mouth', and has said that there was only a very rudimentary set of cash controls in place. 'We set about simply recording what was there, forecasting what might happen for the next six or twelve months and really making people report what was actually happening', he said.[4]

After a year in the business Naphtali spent a whole day with Pratt discussing his future and whether or not he would stay on at Visy. Naphtali told Pratt that if he did stay he would help him reap the potential of the business, which would allow Pratt to turn profits of $2 million into $10 million. This attracted Pratt, and Naphtali stayed.

With real information flows in place the operation became much more professional and Pratt was able to delegate to other executives in a way that had not previously been possible. He also began to understand the financial muscle he was developing, making it possible to buy the paper machines he needed to develop the business, revolutionise the industry and compete in the finance markets as the 1980s progressed.

Naphtali was able to rejoin the Collins Street world he missed in September 1982 when Visy bought a building on the corner of King and Collins Streets in Melbourne's CBD, giving the company, which now employed 500 people, a visible presence in the finance world. Around that time Richard set out to move beyond manufacturing with the formation of Pratt &

Co Financial Services, a move he would later regret. He also began a love affair with the US that would last the rest of his life, buying an apartment in the Sherry-Netherland Hotel on Fifth Avenue.

In the early 1980s Pratt had his first encounter with public controversy, being named, along with hundreds of other businessmen, in the McCabe-Lafranchi report to the Victorian Government as having been a director of companies that were indulging in what famously became known as 'bottom of the harbour' tax-avoidance schemes. These schemes became a major political issue after the Fraser Government introduced retrospective legislation making them illegal. Pratt chose not to run with the argument that what he had done had been legal at the time he did it, rather he said, 'I'm terribly sorry that I got involved in something that, all of a sudden, became a serious moral issue'.[5]

Interestingly, Richard showed some reticence about his business career around this period. As he sat having his portrait painted by well-known artist Clifton Pugh he was asked by an onlooker whether he really loved what he did. 'Not really', he replied, 'But I'm programmed to do it … I think I'd love to run theatre restaurants'.[6]

When Bob Hawke's Labor government was elected in 1983 it set a course that would result in a massive restructuring of the Australian economy in ways that no-one could have imagined. Foreign exchange controls were dropped, the currency was floated, and the financial system was deregulated, allowing foreign banks to set up shop. Treasurer Paul Keating took a sledgehammer to the tariff wall surrounding Australian industry, saying that without a robust industrial rebirth the country would become a 'banana republic'.

For the first time Australian finance markets were flooded with cheap cash borrowed overseas and a new breed of corporate raider emerged, targeting the old industrial fiefdoms of the pre-deregulation era, buying them in stock market raids and flogging off bits and pieces to make a profit. Some, like Alan Bond and Foster's Brewing chief John Elliott, would create massive new international empires that would collapse or be sold off as recession struck early in the next decade.

As the 1980s wore on Visy expanded, installing more paper mills and buying box factories, while the industry rationalised in the new era unleashed by Hawke and Keating. Richard continued to build market share, and by late in the decade Visy was estimated to hold forty per cent of the $900 million box market. By 1988 Richard was ranked Australia's sixth richest person, with a fortune estimated at $540 million.

At the same time Pratt's restless desire for growth had seen him take two new directions. His fascination with the US had manifested with the purchase of two box factories, one in New York and one in New Jersey, along with an old paper mill in Macon, Georgia that used timber as its feedstock, which Pratt bought for $225 million. He also dabbled in the media, buying the *Australian Jewish News* and backing a magazine published out of Israel called *The Jerusalem Report*. He famously also floated the idea of buying the *New York Times*, though this idea never bore fruit.

Pratt stepped out of the private company space and onto the stock market by floating the Battery Group, which held his expanding interests in the financial sector. The Macon mill was also held in a listed vehicle called OVS Corp. Battery hit the stock market boards in April 1987, just six months before the massive stock market crash that would put paid to many of the paper shuffling entrepreneurs who had dominated the financial world in the previous few years. Some estimates had Battery valued at as much as $400 million prior to the crash, which was not bad for a company worth only $4 million in early 1986. Richard Pratt held a fifty-two per cent share. Among Battery's major assets were the Occidental life insurance group (which had about 100 000 policyholders), purchased in 1987 for $105 million, and Royal Life, purchased for $35 million after the September 1987 stock market crash.

All these moves became problematic for Pratt. The box factories proved unprofitable and the Macon mill was in-efficient, relying on old technology and requiring major investment to turn it around. The great crash changed the game dramatically in the finance sector, turning Battery's results from a profit to only breaking even.

There was movement in the packaging industry, as well. Richard joined forces with BTR Nylex, led by well-known industrialist Alan Jackson, in a $1.6 billion takeover of glass packaging group ACI early in 1988. A few months later BRT, which was sixty-two per cent owned by its UK parent, got Foreign Investment Review Board permission to take all of ACI, and Pratt Group sold its stake leaving BTR with 100 per cent.

The publicly listed Amcor group (which had changed its name from APM in 1986) was not standing still either. Its managing director Stan Wallis had launched a three-pronged growth strategy based on the purchase of Containers Ltd. Amcor expanded into the production of plastic bottles and metal cans, began offshore packaging in North America and Asia, and built two new state-of-the-art box plants at Smithfield in Sydney and Scoresby in Melbourne.

This meant trouble for Visy as the new plants lacked customers and Wallis launched a price war to win them. Amcor cut the price of cardboard boxes early in 1988, forcing Visy and Smorgon to follow suit. Red ink was soon flowing, with Amcor and Visy losing around $60 million each by late 1989, and Smorgon also bleeding heavily to the tune of $25 million. Finally, a truce was called in September 1989 with Smorgon agreeing to sell its box plants to Amcor and Visy and leave the industry. Regulators did not allow competitors to buy Smorgon's paper machines, so these were sold for scrap or to offshore sources.

All this had come at a terrible time for Richard Pratt. Visy had debts of around $700 million and with interest rates climbing into the sky the bankers were getting worried. Problems in the US operations and at the Battery Group did not help either. OVS was eventually privatised by Pratt for $147 million and the Macon mill sold, with Richard vowing never to run plants with old machinery again. However, while Visy's first American experience was not a profitable one, it did give the company the understanding it needed to eventually succeed in the US market.

Back in Australia things were getting even worse for Pratt. Battery Group was labouring under debts and its banks, primarily the Commonwealth and ANZ, were asking for repayments of about $25 million by mid October 1990. With the economy and the property market starting to slide as a result of the fallout from the 1987 stock market crash and high interest rates, Battery looked to cash up by selling off its assets.

Heath Holdings, an unknown company fronted by a man who called himself Peter Davis, offered Battery $130 million for two of its insurance companies, Regal and Occidental. Davis claimed he was representing American interests who wanted to get a stake in the Australian insurance industry. Pratt later said that things were so tough at that time that he would have done 'business with the devil to get those life insurance companies sold'.[7]

Initial negotiations with Heath Holdings led to plans for the sale to be completed, and settlement was arranged. A down payment of $65 million was agreed on, to be followed a couple of weeks later by the rest. Then, in one of the most bizarre episodes in Australian corporate history, the down payment was discovered to have come not from mystery US investors, but from the statutory funds of Regal and Occidental. The rest of the sale money never appeared, the sale collapsed and Peter Davis turned out to be Phillip Kingston Carver, a man later described by Justice Francis Gilbert Dyett as 'one of the most devious, plausible and manipulative confidence tricksters the business world in this country has ever encountered'.[8] Carver eventually received five-and-a-half years jail time for his part in the scam.

The sorry tale ended with Regal and Occidental suing twenty parties to the saga for the missing $65 million. The case itself was estimated to have cost each party $30 million, and in the end all parties to the dispute chipped in to make up the deficiency in Regal and Occidental's statutory funds resulting from the derailed sale. Battery then fought another battle with its insurer FAI to win the insurance claim it said it was owed for the failed deal. FAI eventually paid up after much negotiation.

Pratt later said that the affair had cost him over $100 million, but its most tragic outcome was the suicide of Vern Christie, a former Commonwealth Bank chief executive and Battery Group director who signed off on the deal. Christie killed himself on a farm in western New South Wales at the age of sixty-eight, his suicide note mentioning himself and his colleagues as victims of the scam.

While the Battery drama unfolded things over at Visy continued to go from bad to worse. The debt built up in the good times had seemed a cheap way to help with Visy's rapid growth in the 1980s and had seen a major new plant built at Coolaroo, on Melbourne's northern fringe. But as interest rates rose and the economy slumped such capital spending was a heavy burden on the company. When recession hit in early 1990 Pratt temporarily closed two of his five paper recycling mills, one at Reservoir and one at Warwick Farm, as the recession ate into sales of consumer goods.

In April 1990 Pratt told Nine Network's *Business Sunday* program that he would not 'go broke', but his bankers were restive.[9] Visy owed about $700 million to twenty banks and some of the banks were getting worried. Like other companies at the time Visy had borrowed from the banks on what was known as a 'negative pledge' arrangement. That meant the banks did not have direct security over the company's assets, but Pratt had pledged he would keep the debt within certain ratios relating to things such as cash flow and assets. It also meant the banks did not have the same level of security they have when they lend to a homebuyer and take a mortgage over the house. A negative pledge arrangement means the banks ranked alongside other unsecured creditors, such as suppliers, in the event of a corporate collapse.

Towards the end of 1990 Visy needed to roll over its debt, but it looked like some of the banks were not keen to play ball. Were they to refuse a rollover, Visy would go into receivership. Brian Meltzer, an executive with one of the lenders, AIDC, a publicly owned bank providing development capital to industry, came up with a solution. The negative pledge agreement would be converted to a more conventional secured lending arrangement where charges would be taken over most of Visy's diverse portfolio of assets.

Then Meltzer went to Visy executive Michael Naphtali to explain the proposal. He said the concept was complex and had rarely been used in Australia before. 'It would usually take two hours to explain something like that. Once I had finished my presentation Michael got it in about two minutes and said yes', Meltzer remembers.

After securing the consent of lead lender Commonwealth Bank, Meltzer then went to the other syndicate members to explain the solution and ask for their support. Eventually, seventeen of nineteen banks came on side and joined a new syndicate; $700 million in debt was rolled over and the Pratt empire was saved.

Putting the new syndicate in place was a massive task. Every asset in the Pratt group had to be pledged as security to the bankers, so Naphtali and Meltzer sat in a room for hours signing the necessary documents. There were several hundred of them and many required signatures in several places. For a few of the more than 100 entities in the group a Pratt family member needed to be present and in these cases Anthony Pratt officiated. Execution and signing took most of the day.

This period saw Richard Pratt under enormous pressure, which observers say showed. He became moodier and less likely to want to socialise. But where many people would have been crushed by such a load of business woes, Pratt pushed on seeking greener fields offshore. He had learned a lesson and from then on he chose to stick to his knitting except at the fringes, and leave the world of financial institutions and public companies to others.

Following the privatisation of OVS in 1989 the Macon mill was eventually sold yielding a profit. But Richard was not finished with the US and began to look for business opportunities there. In the early 1990s financial experts predicted that the world's economic future lay in Asia, but when this was put to Richard he responded with characteristic simplicity saying, 'I don't speak the language. I think we'll go to America'.

The US cardboard industry was reliant solely on kraft mills, which manufactured brown paper from timber. Many of the big manufacturers had massive forests of their own, and there was virtually no recycling. Pratt decided he would do what he did best. He bought some box factories and put in a recycling mill at Conyers near Atlanta in Georgia early in the 1990s. It was a big mill by Australian standards, producing about 300 000 tonnes of brown paper every year, while Visy's Australian mills at the time produced an average of 100 000 tonnes. He then bought more box factories in the US, gradually building a foothold in the US market.

Anthony Pratt travelled to the US in 1991 to run the business — Pratt Industries USA — and gain his own experience of the industry. Until then he had lived in his father's shadow and needed extra space to grow into his own person.

As Leon had been tough on young Richard, so Richard was on his son, given to directing outbursts of anger towards him regardless of who was there to see it. Anthony himself was seen by some as a 'difficult kid' when he was young. He had a keen sense of humour and was quite whacky and unusual in his approach to life. Later, some saw the pressure of working closely with his father as leading to frustration that expressed itself in erratic and sometimes arrogant behaviour.[10]

Anthony grew in stature in the US and by 2001 he was proud of his achievements and comfortable telling his father to butt out when necessary. In the same year he told a reporter, 'Going to live in America and colonising it as a place for business for the family has helped me emerge from the shadow. I've always believed it's better to be a baron in your own fiefdom than a lapdog in the palace … I'm proud that we have increased America's earnings since I arrived in 1992 from $10 million to $150 million'.[11] Today that figure is closer to $1 billion, with operations in thirteen US states.

Like Richard, Anthony has a touch of showbiz about him. He has built relationships with Muhammad Ali, performers Paul Anka and Burt Bacharach and actor Tony Curtis, who have all performed at Pratt corporate functions at various times. Of former boxing great Ali he says, 'Ali's a marvellous character. We love him, our customers love him, and when he comes into our factories you've never seen anything like it. Loads of staff told me meeting him was the biggest day of their lives'. He has made videos for company parties including one sending up the movie *Forrest Gump*. He also sings but less than his father. He once had a penchant for the song 'It's Thoroughly Rotten Being Ginger'. As Anthony has vivid red hair it is not clear whether the song is an expression of his somewhat perverse sense of humour or a statement about the pressure he was under as the son of a successful entrepreneur.

When he moved to America, Anthony lived in the family's penthouse at the Sherry-Netherland Hotel on Fifth Avenue for the first year. He then settled in Atlanta to be close to the growing business there, residing in the upmarket suburb of Buckhead, where he restored a 1930s mansion built by Coca-Cola heir Conky Whitehead. Following his father's death Anthony spreads his time between the US and Australia. He has been married three times; first to New Yorker Ali Giski, then to Sarah Schoff from Arizona, and finally to Claudine Revere, who in 2009 gave birth to a son named Leon in honour of Anthony Pratt's grandfather.

Anthony had to contend with a very different business culture in the US. 'Business in the US is war; it's not like Australia. Companies literally attack each other. I think this is why so many Australian companies have difficulties here—they expect you can act like you do at home, and it is just not enough.' In order to keep pace with business tactics in the US, Anthony is an avid reader of military strategy, with works by strategists such as Clausewitz and Sun Tzu filling the shelves of his living room in Atlanta.

Visy's second major expansion in the US was in 1997 with the construction of another recycled paper mill on Staten Island in New York. In the mid 1990s the Mayor of New York, Rudolph Giuliani, tried like many before him to clean up the 'Big Apple' by introducing a regime of tough and controversial policing, known as 'zero tolerance'. Giuliani managed to rid the city of much of its notorious crime, while the severity of the city's rule of law attracted condemnation the world over. Giuliani (who became famous as mayor of the city following the attacks on the World Trade Center on 11 September 2001) surprised many observers with the depth of his success. One of the by-products of the zero tolerance program was the removal of the Mafia from the city's waste business.

Encouraging investors back to New York in the wake of this clean-up, Giuliani let it be known that he would look favourably on any entrepreneur plucky enough to fill the vacuum created by the Mafia's removal and enter the city waste industry. Specifically, he encouraged the building of a waste recycling mill at Staten Island, the working class industrial island between New Jersey and Manhattan. Ever the opportunist, Richard Pratt saw his chance. While his bigger American rivals pondered the possibilities and the dangers of the move, Richard was already inside City Hall thrashing out a deal with Giuliani.

By the time Richard had signed on the dotted line to build the Pratt Industries USA plant at Staten Island, he had managed to squeeze US$28 million in grants and tax breaks from the Giuliani administration, a major achievement in a country that is notoriously slow to grant aid for foreign investment. Giuliani attended the plant opening, turning what would have been a trade press story into a national event, as he warmly welcomed the industry 'back to New York'.

Pratt also used innovative financing mechanisms to build the US business. Rather than relying on bank finance that may have attracted interest rates of seven per cent, Pratt discovered that US banks could issue corporate bonds with maturity dates of up to twenty-five years, and with interest rates as low as three per cent. That gave growth in the US a significant boost. Late in 2008 Pratt Industries opened a US$150 million recycled paper mill in Shreveport, Louisiana, giving them total production in the US of almost one million tonnes a year, as well as a growing portfolio of box factories using the output of the mills.

As the new century dawned Richard Pratt turned his mind to further expansion in Australia by making acquisitions within the packaging industry that boosted revenues and diversified operations. The perfect opportunity finally presented itself in late 2000 when the diversified wine company Southcorp decided to shed its non-core assets and concentrate on wine alone. Southcorp announced it would sell all its packaging operations, including about forty factories dotted around Australia. The move created an immediate profit of an estimated $100 million for Southcorp — owner of the famous Penfolds brand — but in the longer term the sale emerged as the first step in a disastrous strategy for the wine group.

After consulting widely with his major customers, including Coca-Cola, Foster's Group and Berri Juice, as well as market regulators, Richard made a strategic decision to widen Visy's activities beyond paper and cardboard. In a stroke, Visy diversified into plastic and cans through the $850 million acquisition of Southcorp's packaging operations, which included canning facilities, laminates and, most importantly, PET plastic bottles (the soft plastic bottles that are now commonly used for soft drinks and milk products). As the former Southcorp assets became a profit driver for Visy, Southcorp lost much of the value gained from the sale to

Visy after spending about $1.5 billion on the Rosemount Wine group and creating a new Australian billionaire in Rosemount founder Bob Oatley.

Acquiring the Southcorp Packaging assets in 2000 sealed Visy's place as the leading private player in the Australian paper and packaging market. The diversification it produced by giving greater exposure to markets away from traditional cardboard boxes was fortified with the purchase of Coca-Cola Amatil's PET packaging business for $180 million in 2002.

Since the truce called after the 1980s paper wars and the withdrawal of Smorgon from the market the paper industry has more or less been a duopoly in Australia, with minor players such as New Zealand's Carter Holt Harvey regularly attempting to break into the market but meeting stiff resistance from Amcor and Visy. Around 2000 Pratt saw that it was time for a change. The natural growth being experienced by the company meant he had to invest in boosting paper production, and given Visy held around sixty per cent of the market it could not do this by expanding recycling alone. Paper fibres cannot be recycled forever as they weaken with age, so a certain amount of virgin pulp must be added to the market each year to keep the quality of recycled paper at an acceptable standard.

Pratt decided to build a new pulp mill in the Snowy Mountains town of Tumut in rural New South Wales, to be fed by plantation grown trees. Making the plan feasible was never going to be easy, with environmental groups likely to see red at the thought of a kraft mill operating in such a pristine region. The Visy group had to get the New South

Wales government and the local community fully supporting the project if it was ever to become a reality.

The Tumut mill was not a clear-cut vote winner, but Richard steadily won long-time New South Wales Premier Bob Carr over to his side. (Carr would later become an unabashed supporter of Richard, returning to journalism to perform a celebrity interview with him for *The Bulletin* in 2003.) The Carr Labor Government was prepared to engage with the project and directly support the factory if Richard could convince them a mill would be good for the state. Once Richard explained that the mill would be the biggest rural investment in New South Wales since the Snowy Mountains Hydroelectric Scheme in the 1950s, it was clear Visy would have cross-party support for the project.

In the Tumut region, where the unemployment rate was up to double the national average, the local population were also prepared to listen to new plans for a mill that would employ 150 local people and another 500 people around the country in ancillary activities. By the time Tumut had become the 'town of choice' for Pratt, the majority of locals—eyeing new jobs and a major injection of new funds—were broadly enthusiastic about the project. Promoting the project to local residents Richard explained that the $400 million mill would use a million tonnes of wood per year to produce 250 000 tonnes of kraft, the basic material used to create the highest quality paper and cardboard.

By the time the Tumut mill opened it had collected more than $40 million in government assistance, as well as a contract from the Carr government that guaranteed it would supply wood to the plant for thirty years. Though large paper mills in the US produce more than one million tonnes of kraft a year, Tumut competes with the US logging towns in terms of efficiency and new technology. In fact, the Tumut experiment was so successful that a further $450 million was spent to double its capacity to 700 000 tonnes per year. Full operation is expected to be reached in late 2009, bringing Visy's total Australian production to 1.4 million tonnes.

Visy consulted with the Australian Conservation Foundation throughout the process of constructing the Tumut plant, making sure the plant aligned with top international environmental standards every step of the way. Tumut is an environmental first in Australia, supplying much of its own energy from green sources, the wastes from the wood being fed into the mill's generators from surrounding pine plantations. It is almost effluent free with waste water from the site being used for an environmentally sustainable irrigation scheme, and water consumption is low per unit of output by international standards. However, there is no way a mill using a million tonnes of wood a year would have everyone's support. There have been objections from environmentalists and complaints from town residents that the mill emits unsavoury smells on certain days, which has resulted in Environment Protection Authority (EPA) fines. Nevertheless, by the time the mill was opened in November 2001, the executive director of the Australian Conservation Foundation, Don Henry, was prepared to share the podium at the opening ceremony with the Mayor of Tumut, Geoff Pritchard, along with then premier Bob Carr and Richard Pratt.

In the forty years since Richard Pratt assumed control of Visy, following the death of his father in 1969, the company has been completely transformed. From a single box factory turning over $5 million a year he created a multinational enterprise with $3.5 billion in turnover and operations in Australasia, North America and Asia. He branched out from box manufacturing into paper production, plastic and metal packaging and investment, and is now the largest player in the Australian cardboard packaging marketplace. In the process he learned some valuable lessons about sticking to his core business, keeping debt under control and only diversifying at the edges. However, these lessons nearly came at the cost of financial ruin.

Chapter 3

Keeping it in the family

Visy is a remarkable beast, the surprising creation of the energised and iconoclastic entrepreneur Richard Pratt. Surprising in the sense that the gargantuan size of the company today is something that was far from Richard's expectations when he first began running the business in 1969. In the 1970s he was heard to say that if he could get the business to make $1 million a year that would be incredible. A look at the numbers today suggests that Richard Pratt could be described as a flagrant over achiever.

In 2009 the company employed more than 8500 people in Australia, New Zealand, the US and Asia. Total revenues for the company were $3.5 billion, including the US operation known as Pratt Industries. As a private company, it is not as easy to value the Pratt fortune as it would be if the bulk of the fortune was represented by a publicly listed company (where you can simply multiply shareholdings by the share price). However, industry analysts would generally put an industrial company of Visy's standing on a multiple of at least ten times earnings before interest, tax, depreciation and amortisation (EBITDA). With an EBITDA estimated at $600 million, this values Visy at $6 billion. Visy carries debts of about $2 billion, so its estimated sale value is about $4 billion. Add to that Thorney Investments, the company owned by Richard Pratt's daughter Heloise and son-in-law Alex Waislitz, and the Pact packaging company, which is in the hands of daughter Fiona and her husband Raphael Geminder, and the value of the Pratt family would be about $5 billion.

The Pratt family fortune also includes the New York penthouse at the Sherry-Netherland Hotel, the Quay apartment in Sydney and the Melbourne mansion Raheen, which together would have an accumulated value of more than $100 million. And there is more. The family also has other property and art investments that have never been detailed in public.

In 2009 *BRW* magazine estimated the Pratt fortune at $4.3 billion, putting the family at the head of the Rich 200 List, and listed Anthony Pratt, who now heads the company following the death of his father in April, and his family as controlling Australia's largest fortune. They were followed by Frank Lowy and family, owners of the Westfield shopping centre empire, with $4.2 billion, Sydney property developer Frank Triguboff with $3.6 billion and Gina Reinhardt, mining entrepreneur and daughter of iron ore magnate Lang Hancock, with a fortune of $3.5 billion.[1] Putting the whole

Pratt fortune into perspective, it is roughly seven times bigger than the average fortune on the *BRW* Rich 200 List of $716 million—or thirty times bigger than the minimum entry level of $150 million for the list.

BRW estimated that the Pratt fortune fell by $1.18 billion between 2008 and 2009 as economic conditions plunged, however this was far less than some others on the rich list. Andrew 'Twiggy' Forrest, for example, saw his iron ore fortune plunge $7 billion in the year to May 2009 as the China-driven resources boom came a cropper, knocking him from number one on the rich list to number eight with an estimated $2.38 billion. Gambling and media entrepreneur James Packer's fortune fell $3.1 billion for the year, while Frank Lowy had $2.1 billion shaved from the family balance sheet.[2] The fact that the Pratt fortune fell less than some other big names enabled Anthony and his family to finish at number one on the rich list in 2009, a feat never achieved by Richard during his lifetime.

Richard Pratt was a resilient man. After the recession of the early 1990s and the ravages of a paper price war and his ill-starred forays into financial services in 1993, he was sitting at number fifteen on the *BRW* Rich 200 List with his fortune valued at $550 million. By 2003, however, he was second only to Kerry Packer on the list and that figure had increased almost sevenfold, to $4 billion. In addition, inside the Visy group Richard has created more than 200 millionaires. This figure is bigger than many better-known banks and stock broking houses.

The Pratt empire is no longer monolithic. In 2003 Richard Pratt began to implement a succession plan that saw each of his three children given businesses then valued at around

$500 million each. Anthony took on the US paper and box business, Heloise and her husband Alex were given Thorney Investments, and Fiona and her husband Raphael received part of a packaging business originally bought from Southcorp and now known as Pact.

Anthony, who is now executive chairman of Visy, has run the US business, Pratt Industries USA, virtually since its inception in the early 1990s and its turnover has risen from $140 million in 1993 to $1 billion in 2009. Pratt Industries USA consists of three plants producing packaging paper from recycled materials on Staten Island in New York, at Shreveport in Louisiana and at Conyers, near Atlanta, Georgia. It also has a range of cardboard box factories spread across thirteen states, mainly in the South and the Midwest. The Shreveport mill was opened in 2009, and cost $US150 million to develop. Visy's key clients in the US are medium-sized companies, but it has had some blue-chip clients, including battery maker Duracell and Diageo, the drinks group that controls the Smirnoff and Guinness brands.

The Staten Island wastepaper recycling mill was the biggest industrial project announced in New York for fifty years when it opened in 1997. New York produces about 300 000 tonnes of waste paper each year, which is more than the Pratt recycling mill can consume. As a result, from 2004 the company began shipping twenty per cent of all the waste collected in New York to China, which lacks enough wastepaper to supply its own domestic mills.

The Thorney Investments story is remarkable. When Alex Waislitz arrived to work at the Pratt group in 1991 he found the company still shell-shocked from a disastrous attempt to diversify into financial services through the Battery Group.

Though Alex was welcome at the company, his skills were in investment banking and at that time the Pratt family was extremely wary of stock market investments. But Alex was determined to change this. He already knew how to handle a tycoon after working for entrepreneurs including Alan Newman and Robert Holmes à Court. Alex planned to create an investment company, ideally a private one, which would be the Pratt family's investment offshoot. He found out that Richard's mother, Paula, had a parcel of shares in the listed paper manufacturer Amcor that the family had virtually left dormant.

Approaching Richard with his idea, Alex suggested that the family use Paula's shares as seed capital for the company. So while Paula Pratt actually put up the money for Thorney Investments, the control of the company passed to Richard. Selling the Amcor shares the Pratts realised $1.15 million and, together with investment manager Ashok Jacob, Alex began working on making a string of investments for the family. A year later, Thorney had investments worth $4 million.

A year or so after the establishment of Thorney, Visy was looking to sell its Weir Paper business in Scotland, which produced printing papers. Alex went to Richard and told him he was asking too little for the business. Richard then said that if Alex could sell it for more than Pratt's advisers said it was worth, then the extra could go into Thorney. Alex sold the business for $42 million, with about $16 million going to Thorney. From that initial capital injection of under $20 million Thorney grew in value over the next sixteen years to around $1 billion just before the global financial crisis struck in late 2007. At the time of writing its value is still said to be around $800 million.

Quietly spoken and elegantly tailored, Alex is a well-known member of the Pratt dynasty in Australia because as a leading private investor he is the central figure in a bustling world of private equity. Hundreds of companies seek finance from Thorney Investments each year but, like many venture capitalists, Alex invests in only one out of every hundred deals that come across his desk. Alex has also become well known in business through activities at public companies, his position on the board of the Collingwood Football Club and his role with Heloise in the Australian Republican movement.

In the 1980s Alex worked in New York for stockbroker Prudential Bache, and then later in the US offices of Robert Holmes à Court; indeed, Alex was the one who had to call the late master financier to explain the full extent of the damage caused by the great stock market crash of October 1987.

Returning to Australia in 1990 after the death of Holmes à Court, Alex began working in the Pratt group and left for a short time after he began dating Heloise. Today Alex and Heloise run mini empires within the larger Pratt group. Thorney's offices are at the top of Melbourne's Collins Street, across town from the Pratt family city offices at Southbank. While Alex manages Thorney Investments in one suite of offices, down at Southbank Heloise leads the philanthropic work of The Pratt Foundation. At the office there is a distinct attempt to display its independence. Alex has Collingwood Football Club mementos on the reception walls. In contrast, Visy is a 100 per cent Carlton Football Club company that even includes a few Carlton players on the staff, among them champion Chris Judd.

Richard's money and Alex's market savvy have created a force to be reckoned with in the private equity market. Alex has said of his father-in-law, '[Richard] is not particularly active. He is very much focused on building the Visy group further and has ambitious plans. He leaves Thorney to me to run. He does not get involved in the day-to-day side of the business'. That may be, but observers say that Thorney gets a lot of business through the Pratt connection. And Richard Pratt always found it hard to resist a good deal, so it was a sort of natural progression for him to encourage the creation of Thorney, as it allowed the channelling of investment opportunities that came his way in the normal course of his business life.

Pact, previously known as Visy Industrial Packaging, is also a significant part of the Pratt empire, employing more than 700 people and turning over around $700 million a year. Raphael 'Ruffy' Geminder, husband of Richard and Jeanne's youngest child Fiona, was a senior figure inside the Visy group for some years, serving as head of recycling and in senior roles in the US operation before taking over the Pact packaging division. He was working as a mortgage broker in New York when he met Fiona. At the time she was working in the marketing department of Visy's US operations.

Ruffy is the least well-known of the Pratt family circle. However, that may change if, as has long been predicted, he floats Pact on the stock market. Rebranding the company was seen as the first step in that process. Observers say that a float may still be some time away, as in the wake of the global financial crisis the markets are not ready for such a move.

Despite being a manufacturer, Visy has some of the attributes of a resource company, as the price of packaging paper can fluctuate wildly because it is effectively a commodity in the same way as coal and iron ore. The same product is produced by pretty much all packaging paper manufacturers with demand and supply pushing prices wildly in both directions. Visy group revenues can race ahead when the key indicators of the paper industry are moving in the right direction. Revenue increased from a little under $2 billion in 2000 to about $2.5 billion in 2001—a twenty-five per cent increase over a twelve-month period. Since then it has risen a further forty per cent despite the dip in 2008 as a result of the global economic slump.

As one of Australia's very few home-grown manufacturing empires, the Visy group is backed by a range of tangible assets such as factories and warehouses. Unlike many leading industrial companies, the Visy group still owns its key buildings, plants and machinery—there has been no attempt to take these assets off the balance sheet. The Visy mills, factories and distribution centres create an Australian conglomerate rarely seen outside the mining industry.

About $1 billion—that is, thirty per cent of Visy's total annual revenues—now comes from the US; however, most profits come from Australia due to the maturity of Visy's plant and facilities in the local market, which are continuing to generate profits long after the initial investment cost was recouped. Separately, profit margins are also tighter in the US, where Pratt is competing with companies that are many times the size of Visy, such as International Paper (which has annual revenues of US$24 billion), Georgia Pacific (with annual revenues of US$13 billion) and Smurfit-Stone (with annual revenues of US$7 billion), which filed for bankruptcy protection in early 2009.

The Pratt empire, though centred on the giant paper mills in Australia and the US, is spread across the globe, with more than 130 industrial sites in operation. It is a privately owned company and is managed through a number of discreet divisions. These are Visy Recycling, Visy Pulp & Paper, Visy Packaging, Visy Creative Print Solutions and Visy Automation. All the divisions are natural extensions of Visy's core paper and packaging operations.

Visy Recycling is the division most familiar to Australians. Visy was a pioneer in recycling, turning what was at one point simply an environmentalist's dream into a business reality. Visy Recycling is now the engine room of the Visy group. It collects waste materials, including paper, glass, plastics and metals, in the blue-topped recycling wheelie bins from more than two million households each week. It has more than thirty facilities around Australia working with thirty local governments and 250 recycling agents collecting and processing in excess of 1.47 million tonnes of paper and cardboard, more than 460 000 tonnes of glass, more than 47 000 tonnes of plastics and 19 000 tonnes of metals annually. In addition, Sensis (the former *Yellow Pages* division of Telstra) has a joint venture with Visy to recycle old phone books, and Visy recycles in excess of seventy-two per cent of them.

Visy Pulp & Paper converts wastepaper collected by Visy into brown paper for manufacturing cardboard. In Australia the group produces about 1.4 million tonnes of paper, about half of which is recycled in three plants in Melbourne, Sydney and Brisbane. The rest comes from the newly completed Tumut plant, which produces paper from virgin timber. In the US there are two massive recycling mills, one at Staten Island in New York and the other at Conyers in Atlanta, which produce about 660 000 tonnes of mostly recycled paper. The plant at Shreveport in Louisiana will produce a further 330 000 tonnes when operating at full capacity in 2009.

Visy Packaging produces 850 000 tonnes of packaging, including cardboard boxes, cans, cartons, plastics and PET bottles. The Creative Print Solutions division (Visy Glama) produces printing and packaging solutions and Visy Automation helps customers partially or completely automate their packaging production lines.

Regulating this level of industrial production at the Visy group is not easy, but Richard Pratt placed importance on looking after the environment. The company has won many environmental awards, including being judged number one in *The Age/Sydney Morning Herald* good reputation index (environment category) in 2003. Still, Visy has had a range of incidents, including six issues that prompted environmental fines from local authorities. The biggest fine was $6000 from the New South Wales government for four infringements relating to incomplete monitoring data at Tumut; the smallest fines were two $1500 fines, again in New South Wales, for odour and air emissions at the Tumut mill.

Richard was also engaged in the debate over water conservation in Australia. His focus on water was sharpened by the fact that the Visy group consumes about 6 000 000 kilolitres of water each year. At Tumut much of the site water is recycled. At mill sites Visy has made significant efforts to enhance the environment. At its Coolaroo mill in Melbourne, Visy has created a lake and garden area around the recycling mill and planted 5000 trees. Similarly, at Tumut Visy commenced a program in 2002 to plant about 15 000 native plants and shrubs on the Visy property.

While Visy remains a steadfastly private operation, it has used outside expertise to remain at the cutting edge of the industry. In 2007, in an effort to improve its corporate governance in the wake of the price-fixing scandal, Visy revamped the board overseeing its Australian operations. The company's board includes former Foster's Brewing chief executive Ted Kunkel, former rugby union great John Eales and telecommunications innovator Ted Pretty. Visy's Chief Operating Officer, former Visy division head Chris Daly, is also on the board. Past board members have included former industry minister John Button, ex-politician Julian Beale and former Coca-Cola Amatil chief executive Dean Wills.

There is also a board—the Pratt family board—that controls all the companies and holdings in the Pratt empire. Traditionally, the non-family board was not run with a great deal of formality. Long-time adviser Michael Naphtali says that Pratt would listen to everyone's views on an issue and take their advice into account, and then he would make the key decisions. 'He did not want to give up control on really important issues, but by the same token he rarely imposed his views on really important decisions', says Naphtali. 'He liked to reach agreement, but he wanted to do it in his own time and style without the formality that would accompany decision-making in a public company ... he didn't enforce his views on everything.'

Even as chairman Richard still exercised quasi executive authority. When former CEO John Murphy joined the company in 2007 it is said he almost had to move into Pratt's office to ensure that he and not the chairman had operational control of the company. It is likely executives will have a more clearly delineated role under Anthony Pratt's chairmanship.

Richard Pratt's best-known outside hiring was the brief appointment of Al Dunlap to review cost-cutting plans at Southcorp Packaging after Visy acquired the company in 2000. Known as 'Chainsaw Al', the outspoken and later tarnished executive who fired thousands of workers over the course of his career (and eventually lost his job at the Sunbeam Corporation) advised on packaging strategy. Richard also hired people such as former Fairfax chief executive Fred Hilmer who became a mentor for Anthony Pratt when he was coming to grips with the American operations of the company in the mid 1990s.

Keeping the company privately owned has meant it could be quick to deploy hundreds of millions of dollars to expansions such as those in the US and the $950 million construction of the Tumut pulp mill. It allows far more autonomy and independence as the company is not beholden to the wishes of non-family interest groups. It also means key lieutenants are not just employees, but often family members deeply embedded within the Pratt empire.

By 2000 Richard's wife, Jeanne, and all of their adult children and their spouses had key roles in the Pratt family business. Keeping it all in the family is by no means rare in big business. In fact, every single member of the Murdoch family is, or has been, involved in News Corporation. The same goes for the family of Westfield shopping centre magnate Frank Lowy, or Tony O'Reilly, the Irish media baron who ran Independent Newspapers, or Ted Turner, founder of the CNN television company.

Loyalty to family and business were two critically important principles for Richard Pratt. He once told *Herald Sun* columnist Bob Hart that the two imperatives can get tangled. 'I work at my business twenty-four hours a day, often at the expense of my family and at the expense of things other people, quite rightly, place before work in importance. People ask me how I feel about my business, and I can honestly tell them it's the most important thing in my life.'[3]

Business analysts often see maintaining family members at the helm of any business as a mixed blessing. There are advantages: family members can hit the patriarch with much harsher criticism than he might ever hear from hired executives. Permitting family members extra latitude for criticism is a key advantage of the Visy group. As a billionaire who ran a successful company, Richard Pratt was not a man who senior executives took on lightly. But as Anthony matured in his role as the heir to the throne, he regularly bit back at the boss.

Talking every morning on the phone, father and son got to discuss Visy group business on a regular basis. In one much-quoted incident, Anthony reportedly argued publicly with his dad over a business decision, shouting, 'I'm the chief executive of this operation, not you!' Similarly, Richard would let loose on Anthony in a way that might not have been possible with a hired hand. In one heated discussion over paper prices in America, Richard was heard to roar, 'Don't accept those prices, you have to fucking negotiate!'

For Richard such methods of communication were part and parcel of family business and they accounted for its success. He once observed, 'Day in, day out my father and my Uncle Max sat across a table relentlessly asking each other if this and that had been done. Every stinky detail was gone through a dozen times. That's why they stayed in business'.[4] He also learned basic business lessons from his mother, who he once described as 'the businessman of the family'. Of her he said,

'If my mother were buying a house she'd argue that it wasn't close enough to the school, the church or the shops, it was a bit dark, and the garden was smaller than she'd hoped. If she was selling the same house she'd argue that it was nice and close to the school, the church and the shops, it had a big garden and plenty of natural light'.[5]

Former *BRW* editor and current commentator on *Business Spectator* Robert Gottliebsen once pointed to dangers in Richard's decision to retain Visy as a family business. As Gottliebsen warned in 1997, 'Traditionally the highest risk strategy is to bring sons-in-law (or daughters-in-law) into a large business. It has the potential to greatly increase family tensions, particularly if the in-laws become rivals to the children for succession. As most families know, not all marriages are secure for life. If something goes wrong with the marriage, the management of the business can become entwined with domestic problems'.[6]

Despite this warning, Richard Pratt managed to exploit the advantages of a family business without hitting the rocks that lurk beneath any complex family dynasty. In fact, he aggressively presented family business as the secret weapon of the Australian economy.

Contributing to organisations such as the Family Business Council, Richard presented a compelling case for family-driven enterprises. He told *Family Business* magazine, 'Successful private company leaders have a mission. They also have long-range vision and share their vision with everybody in the company'.[7] Commenting on succession in the same interview, Richard said, 'They name their successor and they ensure that their successor is well trained. They install their successor and hand over power to them while they are still alive. They appoint the best person for the job, not the best family person for the job.'

Keeping the Visy group private was crucial to Richard during the dark days of the 1990s when the Pratt family faced its most difficult business challenges. As the recession bit in Australia, paper prices fell and Richard became embroiled in a series of crises culminating in the Battery Group scandal, which accompanied his foray into the financial services sector. Richard must have thanked his lucky stars Visy shares were not listed on the stock market because they would have dropped like a stone.

Visy's Australian operations are now owned one-third each by Anthony, Heloise and Fiona, and their respective families, but Anthony has ultimate decision-making rights as his father believed there needed to be clarity on who was actually running the company. Anthony owns the US operation, Fiona and Ruffy run Pact, and Heloise and Alex run Thorney Investments. Jeanne Pratt has no ownership in her own right, but has life interests — that is, she has the right to participate — in the operations. The private structure allowed Richard Pratt the paradox of being a very public man in terms of pushing his views and ideas, while keeping the details of his business interests out of the public eye.

Chapter 4

The unreasonable man

Getting people to tell you stories about Richard Pratt has never been too difficult in the paper industry, but one of the most popular tales concerns a visit to the offices of Visy's arch rival in Australia, the papermaker Amcor. At the time Amcor was housed in very salubrious headquarters in Melbourne's Southbank (although former managing director Russell Jones moved the company to much more modest offices in suburban Melbourne). Richard had done an early morning tour of one of his mills and then rushed into the city to make the Amcor meeting.

Entering the Amcor building, Richard mounted the elaborate staircase leading to the executive level. On the stairs he met the Amcor executive. 'Richard, you're late, and you've got dust all over your shoes!' said his adversary. 'Yes,' said Richard, 'that's paper dust—you don't remember it I suppose'.

Richard Pratt, despite his broad and eclectic set of interests, was a man who was primarily motivated by work. His position at Visy gave him the financial and social wherewithal to achieve his philanthropic, sporting and community aims, and it gave him huge personal power and influence in both the local and international community. He used to say that in a healthy and successful life family came first and work second. But like many successful businesspeople it seems that the delineation between family life and business life was not always clear. He admitted at various times that his family had probably suffered as a result of his focus on the business. But they also benefited from the empire he created, and are now playing active roles in it themselves.

Keeping in touch with the factory floor and investing in new technology were two of Richard's most deeply held tenets. When the Pratt group made its first entry into the US market, attempting to revive the old paper plant in Macon, Georgia, in the late 1980s, Richard knew he was going against his best instincts to always buy new technology.

After several months listening to his engineers complain about the 'old rubbish' that passed for production machinery in Georgia, Richard bit the bullet and sold the loss-making factory. Without losing any time, he then invested in a new plant at Conyers, a satellite town of Atlanta, only an hour's drive away. Within three years the new plant was profitable and his staff were much happier working with equipment that did not need constant maintenance.

Learning from his mistake in Macon, Richard Pratt formed the view that no factory should be kept for more than thirty-five years. He thought after three-and-a-half decades any factory would be antiquated and no longer competitive. Moreover, many of the workforce who joined at the age of twenty-five would be getting on to sixty years of age and, worst of all, its customers will probably have moved to other locations. Pratt believed that to keep up with the world a business must not be afraid of capital spending.

In an interview with *BRW* magazine, he spelled out his views. 'Just buying the equipment and swapping things over is not enough—you have to have the people and you have to participate personally in the purchase of the equipment', he said. '[I say to staff] you can have one of those machines but, please, when it comes here, make sure that the minute it arrives you are tearing off the boards and getting it installed as quickly as possible, because it's yours... it is a combination of the right equipment and the enthusiasm of the person who is using it.

'You have to take into account what you can afford. There is no point in saying you can afford a satellite or an atomic energy source when, in fact, all you can afford is a better motor. Spend at least a year, perhaps two years, finding out what plant is available.'[1]

Following closely behind Richard's belief in new technology was a desire to always have the best information. He believed that information on the state of his industry and the condition of his own business was crucial to making decisions. But he never waited for 'perfect information', deciding instead to act on the best information available at the time. He used to say, 'Don't wait for perfect information. Have last month's results approximately right on the first day of the new month. That way you can begin fixing things on day one. Always have timely information'.

Although not primarily a numbers man he put that adage into practice by constantly studying the Visy 'Blue Book', a detailed financial report on the company produced monthly. It listed financial performance and a series of ratios for each plant that gave real insight into how the business and its constituent parts were travelling. He would quiz employees on its contents and want explanations for figures that were not to his liking. He paid particular attention to ratios such as 'conversion cost'—that is, the cost of creating a box and the ratio of paid to unpaid waste with unpaid waste being offcuts.

No matter how successful he became, Richard always kept his eye on the detail he knew was vital to the survival and prosperity of the business. He never lost a sense of proportion, and he saw the need to keep staff constantly on their toes by making sure they understood this, too. After fifty years in the paper business, Pratt still insisted on meeting workers on the factory floor rather than in plush offices. It meant he regularly stood in windblown dusty corridors, roaring across noisy machinery in order to make a point, but his workers knew their boss was not just looking over their shoulder, he was looking them in the eye.

Taking responsibility and getting your hands dirty were at the centre of Pratt's approach to management and leadership. His speech to the Family Business Council in 1997 offers some insight into the way he did business and expected everyone else to. '[The best managers] look for ways to make things happen', he said. 'They don't try to find reasons why things can't happen. They focus on what they want to achieve, not on what they want to avoid.'[2] Employees who did not share this attitude did not stay at Visy for very long. Achievement and performance were yardsticks Pratt applied rigorously throughout the company. Indeed, one of his many aphorisms was, 'Anyone not fired with enthusiasm will be fired with enthusiasm'.

Pratt believed you should manage situations, not monitor them. Monitoring is for technocrats and bureaucrats; managing is for entrepreneurs and business builders. Entrepreneurs get their hands dirty; they take ownership of situations and grapple with issues until they are solved. If that meant standing in a busy factory until arguments about the placement of machinery had been thrashed out, then that job was just as important as meeting investment bankers in expensive office towers.

Likewise, there will always be those customers who are worthwhile, but who every salesperson dreads because they are mean, or highly demanding or even (and it happens) completely eccentric. Typically, Pratt would make sure he personally met both the important and the 'difficult' customers.

Putting heart and soul into business plans was important to Richard Pratt. He did not think anyone should simply 'turn on' management buttons at work and turn them off for the rest of the time. 'The best managers manage by walking around', he commented. 'They're visible and they never, ever, tire of going onto the factory or shop floor. They make a point of visiting their sites at odd times, after hours and on weekends. They visit their customers frequently.'

Congratulating staff in public has always been a principle of the Pratt group. Less well known is a tradition of keeping any criticism of them private. This principle of 'stroking' achievers in public and tackling their failings in private is progressive and sensitive at the same time, and it backs up Richard's regular claim that he put people first and technology second.

Visiting Melbourne for the first time, Visy customers are often puzzled why the Pratt group has no real headquarters. Anyone looking for an office tower in the city with the Visy logo emblazoned on the side will be disappointed. Its head office is in Southbank, but Richard Pratt was never at head office — or any of Visy's other offices — for very long. 'I don't want a headquarters, I want everyone to be able to grow. I've always avoided anything like a bureaucracy here', he explained.

Leading the Visy group operations, Richard was always out and about. He was literally 'on the road' for most of the year. Though he liked to start most days in Melbourne with an early morning walk around his bigger plants, such as Coolaroo, there was little pattern to his days. Pratt used to say, 'During the day 100 per cent of the boss's time should be spent communicating with employees, customers, suppliers, bankers and others vital to the business. Thinking and planning should be done after hours'.[3] His view was that it was the people in the factories, the people who made things, who were the ones that would know — and not be afraid to say — whether there were any problems.

His long-time friend Bill Montague, who runs his own fruit factories, knows a thing or two about dealing with large numbers of staff. Says Montague, 'I remember visiting the Valparaiso plant outside Chicago with him one day and we were going through the facility with all the workers taking it in that the boss from Australia was on site.

'Then we had this amazing meeting where he brought everyone together in the plant and he stood up on a box and said, "Does anyone want to tell me anything ... any complaints or suggestions?" They were slow to get going at first because I don't think American managers do things like this too often. But it was a very useful session, and nobody at the plant was going to forget that meeting.'

For Richard Pratt, getting out of the office and working 'in the field' with staff or customers or bankers or bureaucrats was of the utmost importance. And it permeates every aspect of the Visy story. Pratt got out of his corner and met his people. He then got his people to get out of their corners to meet customers, bankers and everybody else who allows a company to succeed. The tradition has been continued by son Anthony and is still an everyday part of Visy. Pratt hated bureaucracies and felt that too often senior managers, especially very well remunerated chief executives, lost touch with reality and forgot the factory floor.

Intelligence gathering was a core part of management for Pratt, and still is for Anthony and his band of top executives. He wanted to know everything that was going on across his empire. In turn, he expected his top circle of executives to be completely up to speed on everything that was happening in their areas of responsibility. This controlling element of Pratt's personality allowed him to keep up with the daily running of such a vast company and run it like a small business. Obviously he could not do this alone, so he placed enormous trust in people he felt were competent and would perform reliably.

Many of the company characteristics associated with Visy come back to this simple principle of 'getting out of the office'. The legendary Visy parties—at one stage Richard attended twelve Christmas parties every year—are designed to get people out of their corners and meet each other. The regular lunches Richard hosted at Visy in Melbourne for senior staff were held to ensure there were good links between the management, sales staff and factory staff.

Getting people across the business to communicate through the organisation was a task that Richard pushed on a daily basis. 'The bigger you get, the more difficult it is to communicate', he said. 'You have to have boosters to make sure the message comes through loud and clear.' Indeed, Richard had an extraordinary ability to communicate. According to one of his assistants, the boss regularly made or received more than 100 phone calls a day.

His travels through the company were not to a regular plan. He would vary his visiting schedules—not to surprise people, but as part of his endless attempts to squeeze more into each day. A plant visit might have be penned in for Monday afternoon but became Monday morning instead. Again, this flexibility in the schedule reduces the formal aspects of a company visit and integrated it closer to the working day at Visy.

Building Visy from a single suburban box factory into a $5 billion business took enormous effort, talent and guile. For Richard Pratt, what mattered most in creating a business built to last was staying ahead of the competition. In the 1970s, when Visy was making the transition from a small business to a national business, he spent huge amounts of time and money keeping Visy up to date by sending his best executives and workers 'out' of the company and into overseas markets.

As many other companies hid behind the protective tariffs that sustained Australia's industrial base in the era before deregulation, Richard had salespeople in Las Vegas or engineers in the Rhineland picking up every trick in the book that could make Visy a more successful operation. It was a culture of openness that paid big dividends.

Recalling that period, Sam Lipski says, 'You have to remember that overseas travel at that time was still very expensive and only the very top people could persuade a company to invest the time, and more importantly, the money to send people overseas on what were basically reconnaissance missions. There was no way of knowing in advance how valuable these trips would be.

'But people came back and they briefed Richard on what they had learned, and he was the type of manager who would say, "Okay, let's do that. Let's do it straightaway". It made a huge difference and created a situation where Visy was known to be more innovative and responsive than any of its rivals.'

An example of this is Visy's establishment of a plant in the Chicago satellite town of Valparaiso. The Visy paper mill supplies an industrial region of the Great Lakes that is the biggest consumer of boxes in the world. The box business in the greater Chicago market is three times bigger than the entire Australian market.

Another innovative endeavour was the 2000 acquisition of a company in Detroit, Michigan, called Classic Containers, which specialised in supplying packaging to the big automakers such as Ford and General Motors. Visy paid about $15 million for the company that had four factories in and around Detroit. The purchase lifted its US operations to twenty-seven plants scattered across the main industrial belts of the US, and in late 2003 Visy's commitment to the Motor City finally paid off when Pratt Industries USA signed a contract worth $16 million per annum to supply packaging to Ford in the US.

In later years when Richard was 'on the road' he was as likely to be in his private jet as traversing the highways and byways of Australia and he maintained a bruising schedule. For example, between Christmas 2003 and the end of January 2004, he managed to visit both China and the US for week-long trips, along with half-a-dozen visits around Australia to various mills and box plants.

Travelling over three decades with Visy, Pratt learned how to successfully engage with an overseas market. He learned the hard way: an expansion into Thailand in the 1980s appeared to be blazing a trail for Australians into Asia, but the business, which revolved around a box plant joint venture with a local partner, did not succeed. 'That whole exercise was very disappointing', he later commented. 'I was very disappointed with the way they did business in Asia. In fact, I swore I'd never go back in, but things have changed.'

Early in the new century Pratt's new horizon was China. The company has yet to build a plant there, but it does have representative offices in the country to source machinery, as Visy constantly looks for new and cheaper sources of capital equipment. The way Pratt approached his exploration of the possibilities in China is instructive of the way he was able to turn Visy into a multinational outfit. Through connections in Hong Kong, he arranged to meet with Han Zhen, the Mayor of Shanghai. During the visit he met Visy customers and, importantly, he visited a rival mill—the Nine Dragons mill in Guangzhou, which is the biggest paper plant in the world. Though there is intense competition in the paper industry, like Richard Pratt, many in the industry believe in allowing inter-company visits. Interestingly, this principle of openness to visits from competitors has not been dampened by the Visy–Amcor price-fixing scandal.

Pratt's approach to China also showed his enormous flexibility. When it became clear that opening a paper mill there was a long-term project, he began looking in other directions. The burgeoning Chinese economy was creating huge demand for cardboard, and as Visy could not yet manufacture it, Pratt decided to explore the possibility of selling wastepaper collected in New York to China. The analysts said it could not be done, citing high transport costs. Pratt thought otherwise and since 2004 twenty per cent of the wastepaper collected in New York has been exported to China, allowing Americans to recycle at least the packaging that accompanies the tsunami of goods they buy from that country. Even so, America still recycles a far lower percentage of its paper than do Japan and Western Europe.

Visiting the US three weeks after his trip to China, Pratt followed a similar pattern, meeting first with the Mayor of Staten Island in the New York borough where Visy has its recycling mill. Then over the next two days he visited three mills—Staten Island, Valparaiso in Indiana, and Conyers in Georgia—along with a box plant in Humboldt, Tennessee.

Despite his international success Richard Pratt liked to keep life in some sort of perspective and enjoyed poking fun at his own reputation as a billionaire. In a speech to the Melbourne Rotary Club, he joked: 'Two girls are walking through a valley when a frog comes up and says to one of them, "If you kiss me,

I'll turn into a very, very rich corrugated-box manufacturer. I'll have recycling factories in every city—in fact, all over the world! We'll have so much money, we'll live happily ever after, rich and successful." Instead of kissing the frog, the girl takes it and puts it in her handbag. Shocked, her friend says, "Hey, it's just a peck on the cheek! Why don't you do it?" The other girl says, "You can't fool me. There's more money in talking frogs than corrugated boxes!"'[4]

Encouraging and inspiring staff, both at home and in the international outfits, has always been a top priority at Visy, part of a tradition dating back to Leon Pratt. The Pratts know that small gestures that show the company cares about its employees are rewarded with long-term loyalty. During his first visit for 2004 to the US, Richard made sure the 'Visybird' (his private jet) called in to Brisbane on the way from Melbourne to Los Angeles to collect one of his leading factory managers, Mick Turner. At the time, Turner was about to tour US mills as a precursor to moving to New York as a senior Pratt Industries manager.

Similarly, on the way back from the US in Tennessee, Richard collected Stephen James, an Australian consulting engineer who had been overseeing Pratt Industries plant developments. Richard gave Stephen a free ride home, saving the executive (and his teenage daughter) about $5000 in plane fares and taking the opportunity to be briefed on Stephen's work in the US.

Despite the trend in Australian and overseas markets of depersonalising business with creations such as online bidding for business contracts, and 'webinars' or video conferences, Richard was certain that business would always come down to 'face-to-face' negotiations and ideally those negotiations should be with people you already know. As he explained in 2000, 'Successful expansion is a function of people, place and product. Two out of three must apply. You're likely to succeed in a new place with your existing product. But it will be almost impossible in a new place with new people and a new product.'[5]

In the US where Anthony Pratt struck out on his own, he followed the family business model very closely. When running the US business while his father was still alive, Anthony was always on the road visiting customers. Three days a week he would fly from his base in Atlanta to visit Pratt Industries customers around the continent. Similarly, Anthony's decision to base himself in Atlanta rather than the more cosmopolitan New York reflects a determination to be closer to customers than his competitors who keep their offices in lower Manhattan. Said Anthony in an interview in 2004, 'My dad has always taught me the importance of relationships. When I was a kid, I used to go around with him in the car when he was a salesman for the business. These guys would regularly tell me how important he was to them and what a special relationship they had with him. It's a lesson I'll never forget'.

Richard Pratt had a peculiar dedication to the job that drove much of his success. Working in a Melbourne-based plastics company in 1964, Julian Beale (later to become Liberal MP for the seat of Deakin in Victoria) was interrupted one day by a receptionist to be told that a box salesman was in the front office wanting to speak to him.

Beale told the receptionist to tell the salesman from Visy he needed no assistance. As general manager at Imco Ltd, Beale was perfectly happy with his existing box supplier and had been so for many years. Some minutes later the receptionist returned to say the salesman was sitting in the foyer grandly suggesting he would not leave without a meeting.

'That's fine', said Beale. 'He'll go away eventually.' A few hours later Beale was walking through reception when, to his surprise, the salesman from Visy was still waiting for him.

Announcing himself as Richard Pratt, the salesman launched upon Julian Beale extolling the virtues of Visy products. Beale was so taken aback with Pratt's persistence, he suggested the two men go for lunch together. It turned out to be a very long lunch: by the time it was over, the Beale family business was in the Visy order book. Moreover, Beale had a new friend—thirty years later Richard Pratt repaid the friendship when he hosted the engagement party between Beale's daughter, Debbie, and union leader Bill Shorten at Raheen. Beale also ended up serving on the Visy advisory board for many years.

Sticking to a chosen course of action was a hallmark of business the Richard Pratt way. As a business leader, he continually alarmed both employees and customers with his persistence. Pratt was an opportunist, but the manufacturing industry is not primarily an ideas-based business, in the manner of, say, investment banking. Rather, the industry is about making something more efficiently, more cheaply and of better quality than your competitors, who are often trying to do exactly the same thing. That requires a constant commitment and persistence that often appears unreasonable. 'It's so easy for people to take easy options', he has said. 'I despise being bored and having nothing to do, so I fill up my life as much as possible.'[6]

Trotting out folksy aphorisms was one of Richard Pratt's abiding passions. These included old Yiddish sayings or his own made-up lines such as, 'You don't know what you don't know until you know it', the title of a collection of quotes put together for his sixtieth birthday by Visy's Director of Sustainability and long-serving Pratt family confidant Tony Gray and former Visy adviser Stephen Webster.

Standing out from this substantial selection of adages is one from literature that Richard Pratt commented was the quote he lived by: 'The reasonable man adapts himself to the world; the unreasonable one persists in trying to adapt the world to himself. Therefore, all progress depends on the unreasonable man'. Interestingly, the quote is from the playwright George Bernard Shaw, a lifelong socialist who was the very opposite of a successful industrialist.

But a closer look at Shaw's life story shows parallels that could inspire only someone like Richard Pratt. Shaw is known now as the larger-than-life literary figure who seemed to live forever—1856 to 1950—and who was known as 'the most famous man in the world' by the time he died. But less known is the boy from the regions (Shaw lived in Dublin and worked as a draper's assistant before emigrating to London) who led an early career marked more by persistence than anything else. Shaw struggled for years as a critic and wrote no less than four unsuccessful novels before writing more than fifty plays.

Answering questions in an interview with Richard Yallop of *The Age* in 1998 Richard gave one of his most revealing responses to a journalist's question about his leadership style. 'I have unreasonable expectations', Richard said. 'It involves taking hard options, working longer hours, and pushing yourself harder to achieve these unreasonable expectations, against all kinds of adversity.'[7]

Richard's penchant for being unreasonable did not always produce the results he wanted. On one occasion he left Los Angeles in the morning bound for New York, hoping to arrive that afternoon before 3.30 just in time to squeeze in a trip out to his Staten Island mill in the late afternoon. His plan was to leave the New Jersey airfield and cross to Staten Island in the relatively calm Sunday afternoon traffic. After the mill visit, Richard was to return to Manhattan for a dinner at his hotel with some business associates.

Leaving Los Angeles half an hour later than planned due to a foul-up with transport, it was clear the itinerary for the day was impossible ... at least for anyone except Richard. Though the idea of circling New York and visiting a factory inside two hours to be back and changed for dinner was preposterous, Richard refused to give up on it. Throughout the journey to New York he watched the speedometer ticking on the flight screen, seeking signals the plane might arrive early. Everyone stuck to the plan.

Out in New Jersey, Anthony Pratt and his US chief executive Helmut Konecsny waited in a grim winter's afternoon at the forlorn airfield. It was only when Richard saw the figures on the runway standing in a foot of snow that he finally accepted the trip to Staten Island was impossible. Asked later why he pushed the whole enterprise so hard that afternoon in the snow he said simply, 'I just try to squeeze as much as I can into every day'.

Luis Henao, a young South American–born executive who has worked for more than a decade with the Pratt group in the US, says he believes the constant stream of unreasonable expectations set by Richard across the company has propelled Visy and its executives to achieve things they would never have considered in the first place.

Luis was a graduate engineer working in Macon, Georgia, when the Pratt group took over the company that employed him in the late 1980s. Luis stayed with the company, intrigued by what the Australian management might make of the enterprise. After hearing the Pratt family were closing down the factory and opening a new high-tech mill in Conyers, Luis was impressed that the Australian owners were willing to take such a big risk and put faith in the same staff with the new technology.

'Then I found myself designing some important systems at the Conyers mill and I was quite young at the time', Luis recalls. 'I did not have much experience, but I knew the cost of what I wanted to do was several million dollars, and I had to say to everybody, "This is what we have to spend if we want to do it properly".

'We had a big meeting and everyone was there when I put forward the proposal. After my presentation, everyone was silent—nobody wanted to be the first to say, "Let's spend all this money on this guy's bright idea". Well, of course, everyone turned to Richard at the top of the table … and he says in this slow measured voice, "Well, I'll do it. I'm prepared to pay for Luis's education". I tell you, it brought the house down; he backed me and I'll never forget that. I'm still here more than a decade later.'

Inside Visy 'unreasonable ideas' will always be supported by a persistent strategy led from the top by pursuing a strategy set by the company founder who discovered that persistence pays when he was selling boxes in Victoria nearly half a century ago. The effect of this strategy was that people had to take all ideas seriously. Sam Lipski recalls a conversation that occurred after the two men had added the highly respected *Jerusalem Report* magazine to Richard's press interests, which at the time included the *Australian Jewish News*. 'One morning, Richard walked into the office and he said, "Sam, what would it take to buy the *New York Times*? If we bought it I wonder what could we do with it". I sat there stunned. We never bought it, of course, but at the time I had to respond seriously, you know. If it was anyone else you'd say they must be joking, but with Richard because of this unreasonable expectation and persistence, anything is possible.'

Running a global business without any professional qualifications is what you might call a challenge. Yet this was the situation Richard Pratt had been in for many years. He began studying for a commerce degree in the 1950s but he never finished it. Neither an accountant nor a lawyer, Pratt was a street-smart entrepreneur who knew that he had to surround himself with the best people. More importantly, for the top jobs at Visy he believed he had to hire people smarter than himself. 'If you don't know, get help', Pratt has commented. 'Only stupid people don't ask questions or don't ask for help when they need it.'[8]

Surrounding Pratt at the helm of Visy was a cast of characters that often resembled a royal court, with Richard as king at the centre. Over the years, he assembled a circle of strategists, managers, engineers, 'numbers people', intellectuals, media professionals, even entertainers, who combined to underpin the global enterprise. In reality, working for Visy is a bit like the Eagles' song, 'Hotel California', says one of Pratt's former senior advisers—you can check out any time you like, but you can never leave. Dozens of executives have worked for Richard Pratt more than once. He never lost contact with his best people, and would regularly hire them more than once, especially on specific projects. This allowed him to have a ready source of expertise outside the company that could be drawn on if necessary.

Though he built a reputation as a single-minded entrepreneur who ran his empire with a firm hand, Pratt was a willing listener. He constantly sought advice on every aspect of his business. At the strategic level, he hired a string of chief executives, most notably the former boss of Transfield Defence Systems, John White, in the mid 1990s. However, the most enduring CEOs have been internal recruits, such as former chief executive Harry Debney (who it should be noted resigned over the price-fixing scandal with Amcor). Visy's current operations chief is Chris Daly, an executive with a strong history at Visy.

Often Pratt hired people for special assignments or to sort out set situations. He could be quite combative when it came to industrial relations, which seems to have been company policy at times, and he regularly struck controversy. In the 1990s he lost much goodwill with the union movement when he hired the notorious US executive 'Chainsaw Al' Dunlap to reform work practices in Visy factories.

He also lost goodwill through his association with Stephen Webster, an American naval historian who emerged as a key labour relations strategist at Visy. Webster became something of a punching bag within media circles following his later involvement with Chris Corrigan and the bitter dispute with dockworkers in 1998.

Creating less controversy than the industrial relations appointments, Pratt also used the former Fairfax chief executive and current President and Vice Chancellor of the University of New South Wales, Fred Hilmer, as a strategic adviser. Ashok Jacob, one of the key operators behind the Packer empire and currently an adviser to James Packer, has also been a strategic adviser.

Accumulating a network of contacts throughout his working life, Pratt was able to hand-pick the best people for almost any task. In legal affairs he had former Minter Ellison lawyer Robert Kaye by his side for almost every meeting of importance. Likewise, for personal legal issues he had Mark Leibler, the well-known partner at Melbourne law group Arnold Bloch Leibler. The firm's Leon Zweir was Pratt's very public legal counsel during the price-fixing scandal and subsequent criminal charges that were dropped only one day before his death.

Building a good relationship with the media was always a priority for Richard Pratt. Visy's interests spread across so many areas and Pratt himself got involved in so many issues that there was no escape from the media spotlight. This was particularly so in the early 2000s when his affair with Shari-Lea Hitchcock and the price-fixing scandal came to light. A private public man, at times he resented what he considered the unwarranted intrusion into his private life. However, cultivating and understanding the world of journalism was one of his ongoing objectives, and former journalist Jeanne helped enormously in this task.

Inside the Pratt empire there is a circle of former journalists who can offer advice on almost any area of business and politics. Sam Lipski, Chief Executive of The Pratt Foundation, is a former editor of the *Australian Jewish News* and was a writer with *The Bulletin*. Keeping in touch with cultural issues, Richard had Sam Lipski—a high school contemporary, former editor-in-chief of the *Australian Jewish News* and now chief executive of The Pratt Foundation. Lipski, an expert on Jewish affairs and Middle Eastern politics, was Pratt's 'eyes and ears' on cultural issues. He also attends important conferences for Visy, reporting back his observations on political and economic trends. Tony Gray, Visy's Director of Sustainability, is a former writer with *BRW* magazine and reporter with *The Sydney Morning Herald*. In the US Michael O'Regan, a former New York correspondent for Sydney's *Daily Telegraph*, is now an in-house press adviser to Anthony Pratt.

Beyond this immediate circle Richard Pratt could also call upon Ian Perkin, a former business editor of the *South China Morning Post* in Hong Kong, who worked as a press adviser for Visy in the 1980s. Twenty years later the relationship was still paying dividends to Visy as Perkin helped organise a number of key meetings in China during Pratt's trip in 2004. Similarly, Richard hired people on specific projects: former *BRW* writer Tim Duncan worked as a communications consultant at Swinburne University, while former *Australian Financial Review* columnist Rowenna Stretton worked as a communications consultant at the Victorian Arts Centre.

Working at the Victorian Arts Centre Trust as chairman in the mid 1990s, Pratt hit a brick wall with some of the arts elite who were opposed to both his style and his desire to bring a more commercial approach to the organisation. His response was to bring in Ian Allen—a former electricity industry expert—to be his eyes and ears and to develop ideas on boosting revenue and cutting expenses.

Hiring people smarter than yourself means you have to be able to handle those people once they get inside the company, especially in meetings. Pratt knew the power of having effective meetings between smart executives, and the utter waste of time they could be when they descended into trench warfare. On balance, Pratt believed meetings could be very effective for getting things done, and he discreetly allowed executives to let off steam if the process got the desired results. As he joked, 'If our competitors knew everything we discussed in our meetings, they'd be more confused than ever'. More seriously, Pratt explained, 'Bad meetings can produce good results, especially if you include people who want the same objectives but have different ways of getting them'. In other words, if you hire smart people, do not expect them to be quiet and listen to silly suggestions; they will have strong opinions and the trick is to harness the best ideas and use them to make a better company.

Managing meetings successfully was a daily task for Pratt. Generally, he liked to have his engineers and finance people at the top of the table. In business dealings, he relied heavily on lawyers—especially lawyers who could find a way to get things done, rather than lawyers who created obstacles to progress. He liked lively meetings and believed people who did not contribute to a meeting had no reason to be in the room. He also believed meetings were a way of getting to know how people were really performing and, importantly, that meetings were a method of getting views from staff on management standards.

Despite Richard Pratt's penchant for hiring smart operators, he has always let it be known he was not impressed with managers who spent more time getting press for themselves than they did on getting results inside the company. Bearing this in mind, it is no surprise that few people outside the paper and packaging industry could name the Visy group Chief Operating Officer, Chris Daly, who keeps a low profile in the press but is recognised as a very effective executive. If you work for Visy, no matter how bright your star, you had better remember your place in the larger operation. Pratt did not want to employ yes-men, nor did he want people who were out for themselves, as opposed to working for the interests of the organisation. He did not suffer fools, and demanded that his team be on top of their areas of expertise.

But Richard Pratt did not live for work alone. He saw success as something to be enjoyed and celebrated with family, staff, business associates and friends. One of his favourite adages was 'celebrate your success', and he did so with parties, a lavish lifestyle and passionate contribution to causes, issues and organisations he felt were important. He judged others by how they acted and what they produced; people had to do positive things with the fruits of their success. He was dismissive of those he felt rested on their laurels or did not contribute generously to society.

Pratt was driven by a peculiar ambition and energy that made him the restless, successful entrepreneur that he was. It got him out of bed at 5.00 am to tour his factories, even when he was ill. It made him push into new ventures that others would not have considered, and gave him the drive to follow through and succeed. It made him a great networker and a generous and engaging friend, father and boss. It also made him a hard taskmaster, and at times difficult, overbearing and moody.

It is hard to know exactly what motivated him, but it appears to be a mixture of insecurity derived from his refugee background and boundless energy that constantly needed an outlet. His desire to find acceptance within and have an influence on the community in which he had made his home went hand in hand with a desire to create a dynasty so his family would reap the benefits of his achievements.

Chapter 5

Working five to nine

Throwing a big party might be a once-a-year event at most companies, but inside the Visy group it is a regular feature of the business calendar. Pratt parties, complete with acrobats, dancers, singers and models, are legendary. These events work a treat by making people feel special in an industry where most spend their days talking about the relatively colourless world of paper and packaging. Indeed, the Pratt family has a long tradition of celebrating its successes not only with increased profits for themselves and wages and bonuses for their workers, but by throwing no-expenses-spared parties. It started back in the 1950s with the Christmas parties Leon and Paula would throw for their workers and customers. During Richard's time at the helm there were often three functions a week at Raheen.

Networking was one of Richard Pratt's great skills. It allowed him to open channels of influence well beyond the tight confines of the paper industry. From a lifetime of functions, parties, matches, sports events and masked balls, Pratt built a network of contacts second to none. Keeping in touch with a wide circle of people, including friends, customers and contacts, was the nearest thing to a pastime for Pratt. In his early years in business he liked to go fishing in a small boat on Port Phillip Bay. But as he got older and the business grew he tended to mix business with pleasure, putting his recreational efforts into networking at the football, through the company and the worlds of the arts, and even in politics. 'If you're selling something, spend most of your time with customers who are bigger than you are and work to get their respect', Pratt used to say. Both he and wife Jeanne shared this ability to network and used it seamlessly across their social and professional lives. From their earliest days living in Kew the Pratts had an 'open house' policy on Sunday nights where friends and associates could turn up for dinner, creating a networking venue for all.

The Pratt entertainment juggernaut is an important part of the business, with the family building relationships with sporting, political and showbiz personalities to make their parties memorable occasions. Throwing parties was such an important part of the way Richard Pratt did business that for many years he employed an 'entertainment officer' at Visy to ensure his events went according to plan. Cliff Powell was the Visy manager who held one of the most interesting jobs in Australia before he retired in 1999. The job then passed to Tony Barber, the popular television celebrity who hosted a string of game shows from 1969 to the 1990s. Barber likes to tell the story that shortly after he joined Visy he was welcoming a bus group to a party at Visy when one wag on the bus roared, 'Tony Barber ... this is where you are these days. So it's true, everything gets recycled at Visy!'

In Australia the Pratts have also used football as a stage to showcase Visy. Richard was for many years a Carlton Football Club board member and served as president for a period from 2007. Using his footy connections, in 1998 he was able to use the AFL Grand Final as a venue for some very smart public relations when the Pratt family brought along their friend Muhammad Ali to the big game. In front of millions of television viewers Anthony Pratt accompanied Ali onto the turf where the 98 000-strong crowd gave the former boxing great a standing ovation. Connections like that are what people remember, helping to create brand recognition, and bringing a new meaning to the ubiquitous Visy recycling bins.

In addition, Pratt's son-in-law Alex Waislitz is a board member of the Collingwood Football Club, where he sits across the table from club chairman and television personality Eddie McGuire. Between the Carlton and Collingwood clubs, Richard and Alex have wide-ranging links with the circle of influence around Melbourne footy.

This 'footy' circle is one of the most powerful networks in Australia. Former football player Mike Fitzpatrick is now one of the most powerful financiers in Australia having built a reputation through his Hastings Funds Management group, now sold to Westpac, and has positions on corporate boards and as Chairman of the Victorian Government's funds management and treasury operations. Australian Competition and Consumer Commission (ACCC) Chairman Graeme Samuel is a former AFL commissioner, and controversial businessman John Elliott was president of the Carlton Football Club until his forced resignation in 2002.

Working night and day to build the Visy empire, Richard drew few lines between his private life and business life. Until 1995 the Pratt family had lived in a pleasant executive-style house in Eamon Court, Kew. But by the late 1990s they had moved into a different league altogether. Eamon Park, with its ten rooms, swimming pool and tennis court, was put on the market and sold for around $800 000. Richard had his eyes on a much grander lifestyle.

Not far from the family home, perched on a rise at Studley Park Road, stood one of the last great mansions of Melbourne, Raheen. It was once the 'palace' of another larger than life character, Archbishop Daniel Mannix, an Irish Catholic bishop who left Ireland aged fifty. Mannix lived at Raheen from 1917 until the day he died, aged ninety-nine, in 1963. His political influence was significant and he is best known for achieving state funding for Catholic schools and running a successful anti-conscription campaign during World War I. Mannix was also a huge figure in Melbourne's Irish community and led the annual St Patrick's Day parade down Collins Street on a white horse.

Raheen had been Mannix's pride and joy, but it had fallen on hard times when Jeanne Pratt first set eyes on the house and decided it could be a new home for the family. The purchase was somewhat unconventional. The Pratts threw a street party and Jeanne went around doorknocking, inviting the locals. She extended the invitation to Sir Frank Little, then serving as archbishop and living in Raheen, and, much to her surprise, he came. 'I asked him how he liked living in such a big house and he said he hated it; that he had to sit wrapped in a rug when watching television. So I said I'd buy it from him', Jeanne later recalled. The deal was done and the Pratts became owners of Raheen in 1981 for a reputed $2 million.

Jeanne later said she did not know why she bought the house and that initially Richard did not want to live there. Eventually the family decided to renovate Raheen and have the house as the epicentre of their arts, philanthropic and business entertainment endeavours.[1] It was a tough brief. Return Raheen to its former glory but not as a museum piece; it needed to be a warm venue for arts events and parties. Eventually architect Glenn Murcutt was chosen, a move that surprised some as he was best known for modernising the traditional Australian homestead with curved and sweeping sheets of galvanised iron.

Murcutt was assisted by architecture practice Bates, Smart and McCutcheon, and Raheen returned to its former glory. The front of the two-storey mansion is used for most of the family's social events, while a modern wing constructed at the rear, built largely of glass, serves as home for the Pratts and as a venue for more intimate entertaining such as the long-standing Sunday night dinners the family hosts.

Restoring Raheen was a painstaking affair. Some areas needed extensive renovation, while other areas required total rebuilding as they had gone to seed under the control of the church, which could not justify the outlays necessary to keep the building up to its original standard. Forensic work was done to determine the original paint colours and wallpaper patterns, carpets and fabrics were reproduced from Victorian-era designs. Bay windows added to the ballroom by Daniel Mannix were changed into doors to bring the garden into the space and French doors were added to the brick north wall to bring in light.

However, despite its beauty and the benefits the mansion delivers the Pratts as a venue for public activities, some family members felt it was a financial burden hard to justify. In the late 1990s the Pratt family—and it has never been clear which members were behind the plan—hatched a plot to offer Raheen to the state government. Though the offer was never made in public by the family, then premier Jeff Kennett announced that the offer had been politely refused. It seemed the Victorian government was not prepared to take the Kew mansion without some additional funding for maintenance.

The Leader of the Opposition in Victoria, John Brumby—now premier—then jumped into the debate suggesting that the Liberal government had been 'unbelievably short-sighted' in refusing the terms of the offer. However, the story then took an unlikely twist when Jeanne Pratt declared in print that she never wanted to give the house away in the first place. She went as far as giving the impression she did not like the idea of government ownership of the mansion. 'The government would just sell it', she said.[2]

Kennett later revealed the offer had been made a year earlier 'in a discussion that lasted about twenty seconds'. He did not say who made the offer, but then muddied the waters by suggesting, 'As the condition of our economy improves and if the Pratts were interested we may be prepared to look at it again'.[3]

Either way the 1885 mansion—worth about $30 million but suitable to only a small number of buyers—remains tightly within the family grasp. If the house was sold it would represent a fifteen-fold return on the initial investment made back in 1981; however, the Pratts have spent millions on renovation, extensions and maintenance of the house since then.

Raheen gave the family a new focal point for its varied cultural and business interests. Partying with old footy friends might have been Richard's idea of a great night out, but Jeanne enjoys a different circle of acquaintances. Jeanne is the doyenne of Melbourne's art patrons. She has held a string of positions in the arts world, including leadership roles with the Melbourne Theatre Company, Opera Foundation Australia, Opera Foundation Victoria and Spoleto Melbourne (the predecessor of the Melbourne International Festival). In the mid 1990s Jeanne came up with an idea to refresh Melbourne's politics-ridden arts scene. She formed The Production Company to bolster live arts performances in Victoria, stepping in to partially fill the gap left by the consolidation of the state opera companies into Opera Australia.

Displaying a neat piece of symmetry, Visy employees and customers get discounted rates to shows produced by The Production Company. With this arrangement, Richard was able to build multiple relationships across the community, while Jeanne could support a vibrant live arts scene in Melbourne. Launching its first season in 1999 The Production Company stages three musicals a year at Melbourne's Arts Centre, and Production Company artists have included Lisa McCune, Philip Gould, Marina Prior, John Diedrich, Caroline O'Connor, Rhonda Burchmore, Grant Smith, the late Bud Tingwell and Ian Stenlake.

Getting Jeanne Pratt behind an arts funding initiative means things will happen. On the other side of the deal, the Pratt family extends its influence deeper into the community through this channel. For example, when Jeanne hosted a gala auction at Crown Casino in 1998, the guest list included lateral thinker Edward de Bono and music identity Molly Meldrum. A business lunch related to the gala event boasted Liberal Party powerbroker Michael Kroger, Irish media figure Cameron O'Reilly and Rupert Murdoch's son, Lachlan.

As a former journalist with the Nine Network, Jeanne's quiet and popular style and understanding of the media have been crucial to the wider success of the Pratt family, though her influence on both the family and Visy's fortunes have often been underestimated. She is a key presence on the 'family board' of Visy Industries, and close followers of the Pratt family know she is quite capable of representing the family's interests at important occasions. At the peak of the technology boom she surprised shareholders in Adacel Technologies (an investment held by Thorney Holdings) when she turned up to represent the interests of the Pratt family. Richard has said of Jeanne, 'My wife has stood beside me for forty-five years and has always played a pivotal role in the growth of our company and in our community support activities, including particularly The Production Company. She will continue to do so for many years to come'.

Jeanne Pratt's role has always been crucial in the company and in the family. Observers say her husband depended a lot on her opinions and advice, and that this dependence increased in later years. Jeanne is said to have a good insight into people and was capable of smoothing her husband's extremes, and was therefore a valuable guide in both positioning the family in the community and the business world and working their way through myriad situations that emerge in business, artistic, philanthropic and family life.

Although Richard relied on her judgement it was nearly always provided behind the scenes. He apparently thought that it was unnecessary for him to hear her views publicly at meetings when he could also hear them at home.

Following Richard's death Jeanne became co-chair of Visy with Anthony, giving her a larger formal role in the company. However, she is unlikely to be setting the direction of the company as she is not an expert on the box industry. The role gives her formal recognition for her importance to the decision-making process in the company, but her formal vote is likely to be used only in the case of major disagreement among the shareholders — her children.

Richard Pratt's networking activities in the sports and arts arenas were only dress rehearsals for his core interests of money and power. The 'Cardboard King' was best known for his networking in business and politics. Most top businesspeople aim to build and sustain a structure of contacts in the community; few have ever done it with such energy and gusto as Richard Pratt.

In 1997 a documented list of Pratt's political networking activities appeared in *The Australian* newspaper, the article giving a remarkable insight into the Pratt family's elaborate system of consultants and beneficiaries. Donating to charities and paying consultants' fees for special duties came to almost $10 million in a twelve-month period. Richard had paid consultancy fees to two former Labor prime ministers: Bob Hawke had enjoyed a retainer of $8000 a month for advice on 'Asian and government matters' while Gough Whitlam was paid $27 000 for two months' work in the US that included attending business functions.

Paying for the consultancy services of former politicians may be pocket money for the Pratts, but it is a lucrative sideline for recipients on both sides of the political spectrum. In the same period that Pratt paid a company linked with the Liberal Party's former New South Wales state premier Nick Greiner a $4000 fee for work on 'government issues', former Victorian Liberal premier Sir Rupert Hamer received $6000 for work at the Victorian Arts Centre.

That strategy was carried through to the US in a way other Australian companies could only dream of—by winning the services of former president George Bush to promote the company. Bush appeared at some Pratt functions, often talking to the crowd about his two sons—Jeb, then governor of Florida, and George W, governor of Texas and later US President. His appearances served as important promotional support for the Pratts, delivering credibility to a little-known Australian company in the US market. Bush and his wife Barbara have also spent an evening at a dinner hosted by the Pratts at Raheen.

Contributing to political parties at home and abroad ensured Richard Pratt's voice was heard on key issues. In Australia the Pratt family regularly contributes to both the Labor and Liberal parties. With interests across the world, Pratt was careful not to fall out with any political party.

During a meeting of the powerful Australian American Leadership Dialogue in Melbourne, Richard threw open the doors of Raheen for a range of politicians and businesspeople. At one lunch table the Pratts managed to fit then Victorian premier Jeff Kennett; businesswoman Janet Holmes à Court; then US deputy secretary of state Richard Armitage; James Packer; and the American ambassador to Australia, Genta Hawkins Holmes.

In the arcane world of private equity, Australia's richest families ensure they have a finger in every pie. Networking was not just about getting unquantifiable future benefits by making connections with the well placed and the powerful. Constant networking (and Richard Pratt's love of a bargain) means that the Pratt family's private equity investment company, Thorney Investments, has got in on the ground floor with many good investment opportunities.

In February 2000 a typical 'insider' deal came to the market when Eric Beecher, a former editor of *The Sydney Morning Herald*, decided to join the dotcom boom. Beecher's Text Media company was already a successful publishing house specialising in free suburban newspapers such as the *Melbourne Weekly Magazine*. Now the word spread through the investment markets that Beecher was going to launch a dotcom spin-off called Lime Digital Ltd.

Within weeks every major investor in Australia was on the line to Text Media. Eric Beecher was top talent and Text Media was perfectly placed to exploit the internet. For once, the Murdoch, Packer and Fairfax families would not have a seat at the table, since Beecher would want to keep the vehicle independent of the major media groups.

Among the investors who rushed to fund Beecher's new initiative were the billionaire Smorgon family dynasty and the supermarket dynasty, the David family, along with pastoralist and banking millionaires the Darling family.

But once again seated at the top table was Richard Pratt, in company with advertising magnate John Singleton. Lime Digital was the hottest investment in town—it was a media play and everyone in media wanted a part of the deal. Few could believe that the Pratt family, non-listed cardboard makers, managed to get in before the media's biggest players but once again the networking had paid off. Four years later Lime Digital turned out to be just another forgotten dotcom company, but Text Media has become one of the most successful independent media stocks in Australia. In mid 2003 Text Media was bought by the John Fairfax group for $68 million.

Behind the Pratt–Text Media deal was a network with Richard Pratt at the centre. The head of Lime Digital, Anthony Lynch, was a former executive at the Hudson Conway commercial property group, which is associated with Liberal Party stalwart Ron Walker. Walker regularly networked with Richard: they had both been part of the Melbourne delegation to the 2001 World Economic Forum in Davos, Switzerland.

From the early 1990s Pratt popped up in the lucrative early stages of top deals across corporate Australia. Alan Jackson, the tough-minded businessman who built the BTR Nylex group into a stunningly successful conglomerate, knew the power of having Pratt involved. When he made a bid to retain corporate star status with the Austrim group, his key partner was Thorney Investments. Similarly, when Perth multimillionaire Ralph Sarich (ex-Orbital Engine Corporation) needed a partner to make a bid for the portable buildings operation of James Hardie Industries, Pratt stepped up to the plate using Thorney to take seventeen per cent of Fleetwood Corporation, the acquisition vehicle the two tycoons used for the James Hardie deal.

The arrival of the Pratt family on a company register can immediately change perceptions about that company on the stock market. After Thorney got involved with the Dollar Sweets group with a thirty-six per cent stake in 1998, the executive chairman of Dollar Sweets, Simon Rowell, told reporters: 'I would certainly hope to be able to keep the Pratt connections … [they are] the magic keys that open all doors, particularly to people like bankers and brokers.'[4]

Breaking into the American market in the mid 1990s, Richard's networking skills were tested to the limit. In 1996, as Anthony began to expand the Pratt Industries USA empire, Richard took a group of Australian journalists on a trip to the US. Said one reporter who was on the tour, 'I will never forget that trip … ever. If that is how Pratt entertains his customers they would never forget it either'. The touring party flew to New York and was taken by helicopter over the Manhattan skyline to the Ritz Carlton, one of the most glamorous hotels in the city. The group were also taken to Broadway shows and drinks at Richard's penthouse in the Sherry-Netherland Hotel.

'Richard is an amazing mixture of opportunism and genuine hospitality', commented a former Pratt associate. 'There are apartments in Sydney at Quay West and on New York's Fifth Avenue at the Sherry-Netherland, and he constantly opens both of them to guests. Sure, it's network building, but nine times out of ten what you have is a billionaire being generous and opening doors for people who are not at that level. It's a special way of doing business and it certainly works because people do not forget things like that.'

Entering the American market meant that the Visy group had to become highly visible on Wall Street and in Washington even though it was a private company. Getting Visy in front of top politicians was a major challenge. Accelerating the pace of promotion in the US, Richard decided to make big donations to the American political system. Keeping with his practice of putting 'two bob each way' among Australian political parties, Pratt Industries USA donated US$100 000 to the Republican Party and US$75 000 to the Democrats in the 1996 US presidential election.

Four years later, after Anthony had built the US business to a size that was almost one-third as large as the Australian operation, the Pratt family networking efforts reached a new peak. After father and son had put the finishing touches on a US$80 million corrugated cardboard factory in the town of Valparaiso, Indiana, about one hour from Chicago, they decided to have a party that nobody in the US paper industry would ever forget.

The Pratt family donations to the political parties had already made sure that Richard Pratt was on the social radar. A Washington register of political donations revealed the Visy group election donations to the campaigns of the major parties were the largest donations to each party from the US forestry and paper products industries.

'Never forget to have some fun. Always celebrate success', was Richard Pratt's motto, and on a hot Saturday night in Indiana the Pratts hosted a star-studded occasion that is still talked about in the town of Valparaiso.[5] Paul Anka, the songwriter whose credits include 'My Way', co-hosted the show with Anthony Pratt. Richard and Jeanne flew in on the company jet. Muhammad Ali sat beside Anthony with actor Tony

Curtis nearby. Sex therapist Dr Ruth Westheimer hosted a mini-show of her own, while chat show host Jay Leno did a stand-up comedy routine.

Pushing the idea of 'corporate entertainment' to the limit, acrobats entertained the crowds waiting to enter. One of the night's stand-out moments was Anka's impromptu rendition of 'Happy Birthday' to birthday girl Ali, Anthony's first wife. It was a wild, extravagant event and the idea as explained by Anthony was to party, to network and to stake a claim in the heart of the industrial Midwest. 'It's not really an extravagance at all', Anthony said. 'We deal directly with our customers, the box makers, and it's vital for us to get them to visit our sites. Who can resist doing that when they know that Muhammad Ali might be there? We needed a point of difference to compete with the much bigger American companies, and this is it. What other company gives a box maker and his wife a chance to have their picture taken with Tony Curtis?'[6] A similar event was held in 1999 to celebrate the opening of the paper mill in Conyers, Georgia, with many of the same celebrities in attendance.

There is another aspect of Pratt entertainment that competitors find hard to match. The Pratts themselves are natural entertainers. Richard, with his acting background and baritone voice, habitually sang at Visy parties, sometimes with Jeanne. Songs such as 'If I Were a Rich Man' and 'My Way' became his standards. Heloise and, to a lesser extent, Anthony have followed in their father's footsteps by singing at Pratt events.

The Pratt family's hospitality is, as Anthony said, not an extravagance. It is a highly targeted form of marketing and advertising that powerfully reaches the people the family feels need to be reached. They can afford to pay entertainers and celebrities to take part because such events build brand awareness. The family believes this yields strong monetary returns for the company despite the reality that the effects of advertising are notoriously difficult to quantify, especially in companies that are not engaged directly in the consumer market such as manufacturing firms.

But Richard Pratt had faith in his instincts. Early in the company's history he decided that what might have been the Visy advertising budget would be spent instead on building relationships through patronising and sponsoring the arts, sports and other community activities. This approach has been remarkably successful and makes the Visy group a very attractive employer or business partner. Even a casual customer of Visy who buys a few hundred dollars worth of product will be offered discounted ticket prices to major theatre and sporting events across Australia.

Taking a lead from the great industrialist benefactors of the US, such as the DuPont or Mellon families, Richard Pratt saw everything he owned, right down to his house, as assets that could be used to distribute patronage. Equally, these assets can be used to build relationships with anyone else who might some day be useful to the company.

Indeed, Raheen has proved a useful attraction. The roll call of celebrities, businesspeople, tycoons, writers, politicians, bankers and socialites who have attended social events at the Pratt home would probably be rivalled only by the visitor's book at Government House in Canberra.

Richard Pratt had an eye to positioning the company in the sort of social milieu that would score him points. When Visy first started making paper in the early 1970s it recycled wastepaper. In those days it was a pragmatic decision based on the fact that Visy did not have huge forests producing the feedstock for kraft paper mills as did its competitor APM (now Amcor). But as time went on and Visy grew it became a world leader in recycling, with issues such as global warming making recycling an environmental and economic necessity. Pratt played on the company's status as a major creator of what have become known as 'green' jobs. Pratt's engagement with conservation issues ensured leading US politicians with an interest in the environment visited Raheen. Al Gore, climate campaigner and former US vice president, has spent several evenings at the mansion.

By keeping an open mind and speaking out on issues that fell beyond his narrow self-interest, Pratt drew an extraordinarily diverse range of people into his orbit, from corporate raiders to feminist intellectuals. He might have had his run-ins with the unions; he might have even gone as far as hiring 'Chainsaw Al' Dunlap to sort out newly acquired factories; yet Germaine Greer has also graced Raheen for dinner. Greer and Barry Humphries—now two of the best-known Australian celebrities in the United Kingdom—were both contemporaries of Pratt at Melbourne University.

In the early 1990s Pratt hosted a global meeting of the United Israel Appeal at Raheen and the security around the house on the night equalled anything ever seen in Australia, with the possible exception of the Asia–Pacific summit of the World Economic Forum held in Melbourne in 2000.

It was not all about business, money and good causes. At the end of the day Richard Pratt just liked meeting interesting people. When Microsoft billionaire Bill Gates visited Australia in 1998, a function in Melbourne was packed with media and top businesspeople such as the senior executives of Qantas and Telstra. Pratt was there too, as enthusiastic as a young reporter straining to meet and greet the world's richest man.

Networking and socialising assiduously, Pratt accumulated a circle of top businesspeople who were friends and co-players in a range of business and community interests. Westfield Shopping Centre billionaire Frank Lowy and Pratt regularly worked together on projects. In 1996 they tried to set up a scholarship fund for Jewish education in Australia. (The project never got off the ground after negotiations broke down with education authorities.) Both Pratt and Lowy had extensive interests in the US, so the two tycoons regularly ran into each other at Australian functions in America. And both men, Jewish immigrants from war-time Europe, regularly ribbed each other about their positioning on the *BRW* Rich 200 List.

Applying the same principles of patronage and friendship Richard always ensured that anyone who worked or dealt with the Pratt group was well rewarded beyond the confines of mere dollar payments. Pratt would spend big to show them a good time and make them feel valued, and it worked. As one banker explained, 'The way Richard Pratt operates is very powerful because let's say a purchasing manager at some metals company gets invited to a lavish party every year paid for by the Pratt family. One day he considers changing accounts; if he does, that lavish party is no longer on his calendar and the chances are it just might be the best thing he and his wife get to every year. People don't give up these things easily'.

In February 2004 an intriguing story concerning Richard Pratt's jet appeared in newspapers. The story had everything: a drama, a rescue, a billionaire providing assistance to the rescue

Richard Pratt (then Ryszard Przecicki), aged three, with his mother Paula in Poland, 1937.

Paula, Richard and Leon, 1937.

Pola Nominees Pty Ltd Collection

Richard with the rest of the Carlton Football Club's under 19s team, circa 1951. He is in the second row, first from the left. He went on to play in Carlton's reserve grade team, and then in the Jewish community's amateur football team, AJAX.

Pola Nominees Pty Ltd Collection

Richard (in the middle) with his *Summer of the Seventeenth Doll* co-stars, 1957.

Richard and Jeanne on their wedding day, 9 June 1959. They were married for almost fifty years.

Richard and Jeanne at Raheen for the launch of The Production Company's shows, *Call Me Madam*, *Guys and Dolls* and *Gypsy*, 13 April 2000.

Richard and Jeanne's children—Heloise Waislitz, Fiona Geminder and Anthony Pratt—at Richard's seventieth birthday party, December 2004.

Like father, like son—Richard and Anthony at a Visy customer function in Sydney, circa 1995. Anthony is now Visy's Executive Chairman.

Richard at a Visy plant, 11 June 1998.

Richard with former New South Wales premier Bob Carr at Visy's Tumut paper mill, 19 March 2003.

Richard receiving his Officer of the Order of Australia for services to industry, arts and sport, 1985. His AO was upgraded to Companion of the Order of Australia in 1998. Richard returned both medals in February 2008 following Visy's fine for price fixing with competitor Amcor.

Richard and Jeanne at Raheen following Jeanne receiving her Companion of the Order of Australia, 9 June 2002; they were the first husband and wife to both be awarded ACs.

Richard with long-time
mistress Shari-Lea Hitchcock
at Woolloomooloo
Wharf, 2 October 2008.
Their affair became
public in March 2000.

Richard and Jeanne meeting Queen Elizabeth II and Prince Philip at
a state banquet at Government House in Melbourne, 23 March 2000.
Richard's relationship with Shari-Lea had been exposed eight days earlier.

Richard and Jeanne outside their home, Raheen, 15 March 1999. Many of the Pratts' arts events and business parties were hosted at the mansion.

Rhonda Burchmore, Jeanne, Richard and Caroline O'Connor at the launch of The Production Company, 16 March 1999.

Richard performing with long-term Visy employee and customer entertainment manager Cliff Powell at a Visy customer function, circa 1980.

Richard and former prime minister Bob Hawke singing 'Waltzing Matilda' at Richard's seventieth birthday party, December 2004.

Richard with Aboriginal elder Pat Dodson at a press conference announcing the launch of the Aboriginal cultural network on the internet, 7 June 1998. Pratt supported the network through his role as chairman of the Australian Foundation for Culture and Humanities.

Richard, a passionate water conservationist, at Dights Falls in Melbourne, 18 May 2003. He pledged $100 million to improve Australia's water infrastructure and efficiency.

John Bertrand, skipper of the victorious *Australia II* in the 1983
America's Cup, with Richard, circa 1983. Pratt largely financed the
Challenge 12 syndicate.

Muhammed Ali and Richard at a ceremony honouring the opening
of the Pratt Industries' 'Mulligator' plant in Conyers, Georgia,
27 March 1999.

Richard with friend, controversial businessman and former president of the Carlton Football Club John Elliott.

A passionate Carlton supporter, Richard enjoys a win over Hawthorn in the NAB Cup in Launceston, 3 March 2007.

© *Newspix / Crosling David*

Richard takes over
as president of the
Carlton Football Club,
9 February 2007.

© *Newspix / George Salpigtidis*

Richard and Brendan
Fevola celebrate
Carlton's victory over
arch-rival Collingwood,
13 April 2008.

Richard leaving the Federal Court in Melbourne after apologising and accepting responsibilty for Visy's conduct in price fixing with main rival Amcor, 16 October 2007.

Richard receiving an Honorary Doctor of Laws from The University of Melbourne, 28 August 2004.

Richard with Israeli President Shimon Peres, 28 April 2008. Richard donated this statue at the Light Horse Memorial, in Beersheba.

Carlton versus Western Bulldogs, 26 April 2009. Richard passed away two days later.

Fiona, Heloise, Jeanne and Anthony at Richard's funeral at Kew Synagogue, 30 April 2009.

services. A solo yachtsman was rescued from rough seas after his yacht capsized in the remote southern Indian Ocean, and the only aircraft in Australia capable of making the trip was Pratt's jet, which he made available to authorities. Pratt neither asked for nor accepted compensation for the rescue mission, pleased just to be able to help. Essentially the story was also about how Richard Pratt constantly worked to build good relationships across the community, keeping his and the Visy name in the good books with government, business and the general populace.

Building relationships is all about small efforts. As one of the 3000 guests at the Visy fiftieth birthday party on the banks of the Yarra in 1999 said, 'My wife and I went to this amazing party near Hawthorn and we travelled down to it on a boat. We got off with some other people at this little pier and there was an enormous amount of people enjoying this party. Richard Pratt was standing at the jetty welcoming every single person who came up the jetty to the party. I introduced my wife and about two hours later he came past and said a few words—he also remembered my wife's name. I thought it was remarkable'.

A penchant for networking and entertaining was yet another manifestation of Richard Pratt's desire to throw himself into life. These activities allowed him to achieve extraordinary success with his company, and also to obtain a great level of power and influence in the world. They gave him the means by which he celebrated and enjoyed his success, and were a reflection of his understanding of the need to get ideas from others and stay connected. Not least of all, networking and entertaining emanated from a desire to show others what could be done with adequate thought and commitment.

Chapter 6

Giving back

Money, so the old song says, makes the world go around, and that was a philosophy Richard Pratt lived throughout his life. As with networking, where he felt a constant urge to build relationships outside the paper industry — partly because he understood doing so would eventually yield returns and partly because that is who he was and what he loved to do — so he did with philanthropy.

Early on Pratt felt he had a responsibility to give back to the community. After taking over the family business in 1969 Pratt has said that he began by setting aside $500 a month, increasing that amount as Visy grew, until eventually he was giving away $1 million a month. Throughout his life he took the approach that, if someone needed something he thought was worthwhile—be it friends, acquaintances, employees or community organisations—he would put his hand in his pocket and help. It could be a few hundred here, $50000 there or even $1 million somewhere else.

He realised, however, that ad hoc giving was not enough and, like the rest of the business, that he needed to systematise this process as Visy grew. He admired the US philanthropic tradition, where the wealthy, private businesses and major corporations make giving a part of their raison d'être, and so in 1978, at a time when there were very few dedicated philanthropic trusts in Australia, he established The Pratt Foundation. The foundation began as a family affair, but now includes external appointments. In the early days Jeanne Pratt was very influential in its operations and decision-making; today daughter Heloise Waislitz chairs the trust. The foundation's Chief Executive is Richard Pratt's long-time friend Sam Lipski, who is in turn assisted by trustee Ian Allen, a former electricity industry executive with an MBA whose relationship with the foundation spans more than a decade. Tony Gray, Visy's Director of Sustainability, is also part of the foundation.

Sam Lipski formally joined the foundation in 1988, at which time it was still an informal organisation. 'I asked where the files were and was told there weren't any, just cheque butts', he recalls. 'The foundation in the early days was just a cheque book, with Richard and Jeanne writing the cheques.' In the late 1970s it was giving about $100000 a year, but by the time Lipski took up his formal role this had risen to between $3 million and $4 million a year, a significant sum but well below current levels of Pratt giving. Since Lipski and then Allen joined the foundation it has become far more formalised, and has supported areas including medical projects, the arts, education, Jewish life, multicultural services, family welfare, mental health (which Heloise is particularly passionate about), Indigenous Australians and environmental projects.

For Richard Pratt, philanthropy was part of a desire to celebrate life and his successes. Pratt genuinely wanted to help others, was proud to be in a position to do so on such a grand scale and felt a need to give back to a society that had offered him so many opportunities. He also wanted to support causes he considered would have a significant impact not just on local communities but also globally, and he had enough self-interest to want to be directly associated with that impact. He understood that, as with business networking and entertainment, The Pratt Foundation philanthropy helped build his corporate, personal and family brand, and brought with it a lot of personal cachet and credibility. It might have also helped him feel appreciated by a world that, deep in his heart as a Jewish refugee, he always felt did not quite accept him.

Although Richard looked to the wider world he did not forget his origins. His immediate community was the Jewish community in Melbourne, and in a little-reported speech he offered to the Masada College in 1998, he divulged some of his core principles, which stemmed from his roots as a Jewish immigrant. 'We owe Australia something special for its freedom, its tolerance and its welcoming haven, so we have to be generous in giving back', he said.[1]

Whatever his motivations, Richard Pratt's philanthropic endeavours were nothing short of stunning in their breadth and magnitude. Since its inception The Pratt Foundation has distributed some $150 million and is now the largest private foundation in the country in terms of its annual distributions.

Heading Philanthropy Australia's list of top ten foundations in terms of donations for the 2006 to 2007 financial year was Macquarie Group Foundation with $12.6 million.[2] In contrast, The Pratt Foundation gives in the order of $15 million annually, but did not make the list as it did not give its annual report to Philanthropy Australia.

It is interesting to put Pratt giving in the context of the Pratt fortune. With the family worth an estimated $4.3 billion, $15 million might sound miserly, a mere 0.35 per cent of the total. However, people give in relation to their income, not their asset base. Visy has earnings before interest, tax and depreciation of around $600 million, but it is impossible for outsiders to know what the final profit in the hands of the family would be.

The corporate tax rate is thirty cents in the dollar and depreciation charges are likely to be high given Richard Pratt's penchant for keeping up to date with technology. At Tumut alone the family has spent $950 million on new plant and equipment in recent years. There is also interest on some $2 billion of corporate debt, which could account for $100 million a year. Pratt philanthropy may also be understated given that at least some of what must be the massive running costs of Raheen could also be classified as gifts as a result of the amount of philanthropic work undertaken there. While the bottom line on Pratt giving as a percentage of family income remains unknown, it is reasonable to judge the family among their peers. There are twenty-six billionaires in the *BRW* Rich 200 List and Richard and Jeanne have consistently been two of Australia's most generous benefactors and philanthropists, even when they have not topped the rich list.

Giving money to charity is common among many Australian companies, but Richard Pratt believed that the idea of the prosperous company as a benefactor to society was seriously underdeveloped in Australia. Many Australian companies have no significant philanthropic activity at all. In contrast, in the US—often as a trade-off for very poor government services—philanthropy has reached supreme heights with organisations such as the Rockefeller and Carnegie foundations. Reviewing the scope of Pratt Foundation activities across Australia reveals a philanthropy network that touches almost every corner of Australian society, and puts Visy in the enviable position of being able to 'make a difference' to Australian life on a daily basis.

Any hard-headed businessperson will wonder if such time and effort in charity work would detract from the main game of building a great company, but there is no evidence that giving back slowed down the Cardboard King in any way. The family is Australia's richest in the wake of the global financial crisis. Pratt himself looked at philanthropy in a characteristically individual way. 'It has taken the business sector a long time to realise that you can reverse the old slogan: what's good for the business is good for the community—what's good for the community is also good for business', he said.[3]

The organisation's giving has become more targeted in recent years and has changed focus. Most famously in 2000 the foundation moved its focus away from the arts towards the community sector. When this happened it was seen in the media as Pratt acting in a fit of pique following the revelation and widespread media coverage of his extramarital affair with Shari-Lea Hitchcock early that year. However, the change of direction had been planned for some time and was part of the increasing professionalisation of Pratt giving.

Nonetheless it was a tough blow for many of the high-profile arts organisations the foundation had sponsored. Pratt notified the organisations, including the Australian Ballet, Melbourne Theatre Company, Melbourne Symphony Orchestra and Australian Pops Orchestra, that some $1.5 million in ongoing funding would be redirected to causes focusing on youth, indigenous culture, welfare and the environment.

In 2002 Sam Lipski and Heloise Waislitz sharpened the focus yet again. The Pratt Foundation decided to create a clearly defined future strategy and, just like the Visy group itself, the organisation would run to a master plan with clear goals. As Lipski explained in the 2003 annual report, 'The foundation has shifted its main priorities since 2000 from the arts, medical research and higher education to youth and family welfare, and other social needs'. Reading between the lines of the report it is clear the Pratt family's philanthropy had become unfocused and, ironically, it was the poorest and least articulate members in society who were missing out.

Pratt giving may be diverse, but it has one golden rule: it decides where money is spent. In other words, The Pratt Foundation no longer accepts unsolicited submissions, even in areas it considers to be priorities. The principle behind the foundation is to decide in advance what needs to be achieved, rather than reacting to the mixed bag of requests that constantly arrive. Setting clear objectives for The Pratt Foundation introduces the disciplines that dominate the rest of the Pratt family empire. It also allows the Visy group to set ambitious goals beyond the short-term interests of traditional company-based charity.

The overarching philosophy behind the new strategy set by The Pratt Foundation is to achieve more than short-term benefits from charity work. Typically more than 170 projects in Australia will receive money from The Pratt Foundation in any given year. Donations can range from less than $5000 to more than $1 million.

Guiding each of the donations is a principle to help the underprivileged. And so, at first glance, a donation such as $40 000 to Melbourne's plush Wesley College might raise eyebrows. But a closer inspection shows the grant is to ensure that 'financially disadvantaged students' who have managed to get into the school can afford to participate in the school's country camp at Clunes, in Victoria, which is an extra cost for those students. Likewise, a $10 000 donation to the Harvard Club of Australia might seem indulgent, except that the gift is to finance a scholarship to Harvard University in Boston for people working in Australia's non-profit sector.

On reading about a Commonwealth Bank decision in 1997 to withdraw a $5000 sponsorship for school chess in New South Wales, Richard Pratt stepped in and replaced the funds. While not a big sponsorship, patronage economics is not the same as business economics. The cash amounts do not have to be large — ideally, they should be judicious and well timed. In the case of the New South Wales school chess donation, there was a genuine need as the money to fund the program was running out. What is more, Leon Pratt, Richard's father, was a keen chess player in his younger days in Poland, so Richard clearly had a soft spot for this cause.

Richard Pratt did question his own motivations for his philanthropy. He admitted there was an element of self-interest and public relations, and wondered whether it was a way of buying respect, 'But then I discount that', he said. 'You don't buy respect; you get respect by giving respect.'[4]

Similarly, Jeanne's decision to open Raheen's gardens to the public, as part of the 1999 Australian Open Garden Scheme, shows her resolve to engage with the public in a way that transcends simple tax-deductible philanthropy. It was a move designed to share the Pratt private home with others and fitted with the family philosophy of playing a public role in their home city.

Occasionally Richard would blast Australian company leaders who never put their hands in their pockets for charity or other philanthropic requests. At the launch of a new website for the Australia Foundation for Culture and the Humanities, an organisation he chaired in the 1990s, Richard drew attention to the paltry amount of money that went to the arts. Business gives about ten times more to sport than it does the arts, and Richard took to the podium and berated the 'enormous number' of companies that never contributed anything to the arts community.

His move later to slash funding to the arts, while difficult for the arts community to swallow at the time, did not represent an about-face on the issue. Even after some funding was withdrawn from mainstream organisations, smaller arts bodies and Jeanne's group The Production Company were still supported.

The Pratt Foundation giving goes well beyond the narrow boundaries of most company charities. Some of the donations the foundation made in the fifteen months to June 2003 include $3000 to help build the Philippine Community Centre in Laverton, in Melbourne; a $5000 grant to support an ACTU program that helps young people make the transition to working life; a $10 000 grant to the Anglican Church outreach service for homeless people; $1 million to the Australian Red Cross to support rural residents across Australia affected by the drought; $7000 to the Royal Flying Doctor Sevice; and $22 000 to Centrefarm, a horticulture project in an Aboriginal desert community in central Australia.

The philosophy of philanthropy is not restricted to Visy's owners but permeates the company. A staff giving program involves the company matching staff donations dollar for dollar for as much as $10 000 per gift. In the 2008 to 2009 year the program gave around $400 000 to a range of projects. There was a heavy emphasis towards fire relief following the devastating Black Saturday fires in Victoria in February 2009. A wide range of other causes has been aided by the staff giving program, including Melbourne's Box Hill Chorale and global organisations such as Médicins Sans Frontières, the French-based international medical care agency.

Visy also likes to engage directly with the communities in which it operates and pursuing this goal Richard Pratt launched Visy Cares in 1995. The program builds community capital assets in local communities, often where Visy has factories or other businesses. This engagement with local communities was particularly important to Pratt.

Connecting with local communities, the capital requirements for each Visy Cares project are generally financed by Visy Cares, the federal government, the state government and the council. There are Visy Cares projects in Victoria in Dandenong, Reservoir, Meadow Heights, Laverton, Sunshine and Shepparton. All Visy Cares projects are owned and operated by the local community. Negotiations are progressing for the establishment of additional projects in Fairfield in Victoria, and in Brisbane.

The Visy Cares projects include: youth service centres; a canteen, student lounge and study centre at a suburban secondary college; a transition centre for young people disconnected from mainstream education; a hospital emergency entrance and dental service; indoor basketball courts and performing arts facility; and a community learning centre.

In Pratt's home town of Shepparton there are two Visy Cares projects, and it is as a partner in the SPC Ardmona Share-A-Can plan that Visy makes a big difference to the town once a year. SPC Ardmona is a successful fruit-canning operation based in Shepparton that was rescued in a management buyout and stock market flotation in the early 1990s. As a Visy group customer, SPC Ardmona asked Visy to lend a hand with its novel Share-A-Can plan, where the equivalent of one day's production from the SPC Ardmona factory goes directly to charity. The plan involves not just SPC Ardmona, but many suppliers and transport companies that engage with the project.

The Share-A-Can Day produces $750 000 worth of fruit and produce packed in 400 000 cans. Visy supports the initiative with donations of cans and corrugated boxes, and many Visy staff volunteer to help out. Share-A-Can has become the biggest food donation initiative in Australia, and over its eleven-year life Share-A-Can has delivered about $10 million worth of food to the needy.

In Tumut, where Visy spent around $950 million building a state-of-the-art environmentally friendly kraft paper mill, Visy also has been a major source of community funding.

The company gives significant aid to local organisations, such as service clubs, schools and fire brigades, as part of a commitment to the town that was established when Visy decided on the region for its major papermaking expansion.

There was something different about Pratt philanthropy that related to the sort of man Richard was. He liked to use the football analogy of when you do something wholeheartedly you 'put your body in'. That philosophy applied equally to his philanthropic and business endeavours. The truth was that when you got Pratt Foundation money, in some sense you got Dick Pratt too. In the eyes of some of the organisations he was involved with this was both a blessing and a curse. Some philanthropic organisations felt the Pratt gaze over their shoulders, watching that their aims with Pratt money were met, could be uncomfortable. In addition, when Pratt became personally involved in an organisation he made waves by pushing to ensure that efficiency was improved and new ideas implemented. This was the case with the Victorian Arts Centre Trust where he was chairman from June 1993 to June 2000.

Richard Pratt took the arts seriously. As an internationally successful actor, he understood the role of the arts in society in a way most businesspeople of his generation did not, and he saw himself as a cultural entrepreneur. 'The arts spark economic growth, revitalise cities and improve the business climate…They help us to reflect on our deepest concerns and aspirations and hold them up for our examination', he once said.[5] He went on to argue that the contribution of the arts to gross domestic product was greater than most manufacturing industries, as well as the sport and recreation business, and therefore management of the arts was too important to be left solely to government.

Interestingly Pratt also saw significant benefits for businesses that contribute to cultural and educational development. 'They tend to attract and retain the best and brightest in the workforce', he commented. 'They improve their corporate relations, communication and positioning. And they improve their sales and productivity because customers and employees respond positively.'[6]

Richard was appointed chairman of the Victorian Arts Centre Trust by then state premier Jeff Kennett. Kennett had been elected the previous year in the midst of a massive state crisis of confidence, brought about by a collapse in the finance and property sectors. He wanted to recreate Melbourne in part by developing its underutilised capital in education, the knowledge industries and the arts, and he and Pratt spoke the same language on those issues. As Kennett was dealing with parlous state finances Pratt was faced with an arts centre running a deficit in response to the recession, and Kennett wanted someone heading the trust who would bring about the sort of radical change he was bringing about in the state at large.

The trust was effectively the landlord of the Victorian Arts Centre (VAC) and adjacent Sidney Myer Music Bowl, and its charter demanded it contribute to 'the enrichment of cultural, educational, social and economic life of the people of Victoria'.[7] If anyone thought Richard Pratt was going to be a ceremonial-style chairman, they were sorely mistaken. He brought the eyes of a businessman to the task at hand. He thought that the VAC needed a new buzz around it, that more people should pass through its doors and that it was being held captive to the perceptions of people who believed it should engage only with what they regarded as the culturally literate. Pratt had other views. He wanted the VAC to become a 'people's palace', an asset for the whole community.

He told the board at his first meeting in July 1993 that he wanted the organisation to become financially independent of the state government and that when government help was necessary it should go to the arts companies not the centre. He also launched an Arts Angels program, which looked to the big end of town for funding, requiring members to donate at least $100 000 a year. Over the seven years of his chairmanship the program raised $15 million. By the time Pratt left it was raising $4 million a year, of which Pratt was contributing $1 million.

Pratt went about recreating the VAC to make it more accessible and attractive to the general public. He gave the board a much more proactive role in running the organisation, no longer leaving things up to management. Posters of upcoming events were conspicuously displayed, modifications were made to toilets, family facilities and escalators, some of which Pratt paid for, and a coffee shop was installed on the pavement out the front of the building. He boosted the number of free concerts at the centre's theatres and the Sidney Myer Music Bowl, increasing attendances from 52 000 in 1992 to 275 000 in 1997 to 1998, and personally paid for massive flower displays at the entry foyer to the theatres building.

Most controversially within the organisation he drove changes that allowed stage facilities not being used for rehearsals to be rented out to other companies wishing to use them as a way of boosting revenues, and he changed and reduced the number of free tickets to shows for VAC staff. He also instigated more transparent accounting and reporting and held regular meetings with staff to ensure dialogue. Pratt also brought in his own man to be his eyes and ears in the VAC, Ian Allen, who is now a Pratt Foundation trustee and CEO of Visy Cares.

Allen used his management expertise and spread himself far and wide through the organisation, talking to staff from areas including marketing, building maintenance and technical support. He developed a rapport with them, and the result was suggestions filtering back to the chairman from staff on the ground. Allen even used his expertise in the electricity industry to get the centre's power contract renegotiated, resulting in a saving of around $1.2 million a year. Allen's work led to a major review of VAC operations. However, he was not popular with some of the management who saw him as a Trojan Horse for Pratt and a threat. Eventually after complaints to the premier about dual management in the VAC he left in 1995 to work on other projects for Pratt. He was replaced for a time by former University of Melbourne fine arts professor Margaret Manion, but was reinstated in 1998 following Kennett's re-election in March 1996.

What Richard Pratt sought to do at the Victorian Arts Centre was instigate a massive cultural change to make the organisation more accountable, more commercial and more in touch with the needs of the community. His decisions were not always popular with staff, some of whom believed he was trying to run the centre like it was a box plant and did not really understand the governance needs of a statutory organisation. Pratt for his part felt the organisation had been too insular and needed a shake-up, and was frustrated with the slow pace of change. 'He thought the Arts Centre was full of ugly people, sexual perverts and socialists', recalled an Arts Centre official. 'He came in and saw the centre as needing a total turnaround. I don't think he ever fully understood that it was a statutory government body. He was more concerned with the bottom line.'[8]

He famously clashed with VAC general manager Sue Nattrass who, while she agreed with many of his aims, was more consultative and collaborative in nature and counselled a less confrontational approach to change and management. She also concurred with some of the assessments that Pratt did not altogether understand the cultural differences between industry and the arts. 'We certainly had our differences of opinion', recalls Nattrass. But she says she understands what Pratt was trying to do and is still astonished by his generosity in donating to the cause. 'What drives him is that he likes to be respected and I learnt that under that tough businessman thing, he has a good heart. He really wanted the Arts Centre to be the best.'[9]

Nattrass also paid tribute to Pratt's 'wonderful thinking brain' and said some in the arts community can be 'too precious' and 'very wanky'.[10] But working with Richard was certainly a challenge for her and for others in the organisation. She remembered she and Pratt had had some legendary arguments. In one month in 1997 three VAC executives resigned and the word went around that Richard was on his way out. In the end he stayed. Nattrass had already left six months before her contract expired in 1996, to become artistic director of the Melbourne International Arts Festival for 1998 and 1999. Jeff Kennett referred to Pratt and Nattrass's stormy relationship in a speech at her departure party at Raheen.

Observers said that some of the discord at the VAC was deliberately created by Pratt in the way it was in his business. He felt it useful to provoke people to see what they really thought and felt about issues to allow him maximum information for decision-making. The difference was, however, that at the VAC he was not making decisions alone.

Richard Pratt took a proprietorial interest in the VAC during his time as chairman. His long-time friend Max Shavitsky once accompanied him to a concert at the centre. As they were leaving, Pratt discovered only one exit was open. 'He made a few explicit comments', says a diplomatic Shavitsky. Pratt had told the centre he wanted four exits open. And he was often heard saying he wanted Melbourne's taxi drivers to 'bloody well know where the hell the Arts Centre actually was'.[11]

Not all of his grand plans got up. When the Federation Square project opposite Flinders Street Station was being planned he proposed the construction there of a new gallery, leaving the current National Gallery of Victoria building as extra space for the theatre and performance centres. He also proposed a total remodelling of the Sidney Myer Music Bowl, a move widely opposed on the grounds the iconic design needed to be preserved. However, Federation Square is now home to the NGV's Ian Potter Centre, while a $21 million refurbishment of the Sidney Myer Music Bowl was achieved with support from the state government and the Myer family.

Richard Pratt left the Victorian Arts Centre Trust in June 2000, nine months ahead of his planned departure, after news of his extramarital relationship with Shari-Lea Hitchcock surfaced. While he and VAC management still harboured some frustration from his time there, it was seen as a success.

Patronage had grown strongly, fundraising was far healthier, there had been significant renovation and improvements to infrastructure, the finances were on a sound footing and public awareness of the centre had improved. As for the frustrations, well, that was Richard Pratt.

The VAC was not the only organisation to receive the philanthropic and business energies of Richard Pratt. In 1992 he was chairman of The Australian United States Coral Sea Commemorative Council's finance committee, and raised more than $1 million to help fund the council's activities. He served as foundation chancellor of Melbourne's Swinburne University of Technology between March 1993 and April 2000, and between May 1995 and late 1999 he was chairman of the Australia Foundation for Culture and the Humanities, which was later renamed the Australian Business Arts Foundation (ABAF). He began the appointment at the ABAF, which promotes corporate support for the arts, with a $3 million grant from The Pratt Foundation, and went on to become patron of the ABAF. He was also chairman of the Board of Management of the Mental Health Research Institute of Victoria, where he helped raise funds for a new research centre for the institute, and was an active member of The Young Presidents' Organisation. In all these positions Pratt contributed far more than money; he contributed expertise, energy, ideas and connections, and always ruffled a few feathers in the process.

Not that he was averse to giving to sport as well. Visy is a long-time supporter of the Carlton Football Club and in the early 1980s Richard got involved in what became Australia's winning America's Cup battle. He gave $250 000 to the Victorian *Challenge 12* syndicate, which along with Sydney yachting personality Syd Fischer's *Advance* was eventually beaten by the ultimate winner, Alan Bond's *Australia II*, for the rights to challenge the Americans for the coveted cup. Before the matter between the three Aussie boats had been decided, however, Bond approached the *Challenge 12* syndicate demanding repayment of $450 000 it owed him on threat of repossession of the boat. Richard Pratt, at the time in a Hawaiian hospital with an infected foot, was approached by syndicate chairman Sir Peter Derham and agreed to come up with the necessary cash.

The move triggered a wave of publicity and Richard and Jeanne became celebrities in Rhode Island (where the race was held). The Pratts had developed a reputation for their hospitality following a party Jeanne had thrown prior to the cup finals race series at a former Vanderbilt family mansion in Newport. The guests had included Jacqueline Kennedy Onassis's mother Janet Auchincloss, former prime minister Malcom Fraser and New York's state governor. Richard was lorded in the Australian press as the 'Bob Hawke of business'. His ultimate contribution to the challenge likely topped $1 million after taking into account Visy's investment of cash, money, resources and personnel.

In one of his last significant public gestures, in May 2008 Pratt, along with Israeli President Shimon Peres and the then Australian Governor-General Michael Jeffery, opened the Park of the Australian Soldier in Beersheeba, Israel. The park, funded by a $3 million donation from The Pratt Foundation, is a memorial to the last major successful cavalry charge in history. In October 1917 the Fourth Australian Light Horse Brigade galloped six kilometres to take Beersheba and its famous wells, banking on the belief they could ride faster than the Turks could lower their heavy artillery pieces. The decision proved correct and played a significant role in breaking the Turkish defences in Palestine. It was a project that addressed a lot of what was important to Richard Pratt—the victory of Aussie daring in the biblical lands that would be reborn as the homeland for the remaining Jewish population, which had been decimated by the Holocaust.

Richard and Jeanne's contributions to philanthropy, industry and the arts were recognised with a series of national awards. In 1985 Richard received the Officer of the Order of Australia, a feat Jeanne followed in 1989. Richard's AO was upgraded to Companion of the Order of Australia, the country's highest honour, in 1998 and Jeanne again followed suit in 2002, creating Australia's first family where husband and wife could each boast 'AC' after their names.

In 2004 Richard and Jeanne also won the prestigious Humanitarian of the Year Award from the US-based Variety Clubs International. The international award dates back to 1938 and has been won by people as diverse as British prime minister Sir Winston Churchill, golfer Arnold Palmer and comedian Bob Hope. Other accolades Richard Pratt received include the Israeli Prime Minister's Award for Philanthropy in 2000 and the Ellis Island International Medal of Honour, which he was given in 2005 and which recognises the contribution of immigrants in the United States and around the world. In 2007 Richard and Jeanne also received the Woodrow Wilson Award for Corporate Citizenship from the Woodrow Wilson Center, part of Washington's Smithsonian Institution, for their years of philanthropic work.

Richard Pratt's philanthropy was one of the significant markers of his life. He stands out as an early adopter of the formal philanthropic ethic in the corporate world, and also as someone who gave significant amounts of his time and expertise to philanthropy while running a major, growing industrial company. His and Jeanne's philanthropic efforts have been adopted by their children through the running of The Pratt Foundation. In February 2008 Richard voluntarily returned his Order of Australia awards following his admission that he and Visy had been involved in a cartel with rival Amcor in the packaging industry, however his philanthropic achievements remain.

Chapter 7

A European affair

By 2000 Richard Pratt's propensity to speak out on issues, maintain a high profile in sport and the arts, and hold parties and use celebrities to build business and political relationships had made him a very high profile public figure. In fact, his profile was far higher than the many others who joined him on the *BRW* Rich 200 List, which the Australian media traditionally uses as a yardstick of wealth. But Pratt's high profile came back to haunt him that year when a matter he considered private burst onto the public stage courtesy of the media.

Pratt had built his whole life around business and family, so much so that the two were intertwined. Visy was resolutely and exclusively a family company, centred largely on Pratt's own family—his wife Jeanne, the children and their spouses were all deeply involved.

In March 2000 it emerged that Richard Pratt's family situation was more complex than the general public had presumed when seasoned Fairfax investigative journalist Ben Hills uncovered a story about a nanny, Julie Page, who had sought an apprehended violence order against her employer. It was not necessarily a big story, but Hills knew there was something different about this particular yarn: Shari-Lea Hitchcock, the woman against whom the action was directed, was Richard Pratt's then thirty-year-old mistress.

It was in the foyer of Waverly Court House in the eastern suburbs of Sydney that a remarkable mistake was made. A man allegedly approached Hills and, mistaking him for a lawyer, introduced himself as Mr Michael Panopoulos, an employee of the Melbourne packaging company, Visy.

On 15 March 2000 Ben Hills reported the alleged approach in *The Sydney Morning Herald*: "'Has the complaint been withdrawn?" [Panopoulos] asked anxiously. "I have a sum of money for Julie, but only if she's withdrawn her complaint." It was only when he was asked whether the money was in the bag that the penny dropped that he was talking to a reporter, and Mr Panopoulos backed away with a stricken look.'[1]

Panopolous denied Hills's story—there are always two sides to every story. He has since sworn a statutory declaration saying that Hills approached him and misrepresented his position as a reporter, and that the conversation about the money did not happen.[2]

After further research, Hills had discovered that Julie was paid $23 000 in return for dropping the court action against

Shari-Lea. By then the relationship between Pratt and Hitchcock was at least five years old and had already produced a daughter, Paula, born in 1997. Paula was named after Pratt's esteemed mother.

The origins of Pratt's relationship with Shari-Lea are unclear. One story has it that Pratt met the glamorous blonde former swimsuit model in a lift in a central Sydney building. A short conversation ensued and Pratt invited her to lunch. Another story says that they met at a party organised by some of Pratt's Sydney-based friends. Whatever the actual details of their meeting, Pratt and Hitchcock appear to have had some sort of connection since the early 1990s—a connection that blossomed into a relationship by mid decade. This was no fly-by-night affair; it was a relationship that developed into something important for both parties.

Pratt took an interest in Shari-Lea's life and even sponsored her to study law at Canberra University. She was admitted as a solicitor in 1995. Hitchcock worked for a short time as a law clerk for major law firm Mallesons Stephen Jacques, and then for family law specialists Gayle Meredith and Associates, where she was seen as someone with a bright future in the law. After Paula's birth Pratt set up Hitchcock in a $2.5 million house overlooking Sydney's Centennial Park, with a car, driver and monthly allowance also thrown in. Later, Shari-Lea went harbourside with a $5 million home in Watsons Bay. At the time of the legal dispute with Julie Page the court also heard she had somewhere close to $400 000 in bank accounts and other investments.

Shari-Lea hailed from the area around Nowra, on the south coast of Sydney, and was born in 1969. She had an uneventful childhood, growing up with her father Allan, her mother

Shawne and a sister. She attended Bomaderry High School and worked as a cadet journalist on the *South Coast Register* after graduating. Ironically, Jeanne Pratt also worked as a journalist before marrying Richard.

Not only did Pratt take an interest in Shari-Lea's long-term future, he also took a liking to her parents. He took them under his wing, having regular meals with them and buying them gifts, which included a Rolex watch and overseas holidays.[3] Shari-Lea's father even did some work for Visy managing building projects.

The Pratt family apparently knew about Shari-Lea prior to Ben Hills's fortuitous meeting at Waverly Court House. Jeanne apparently knew about the affair for many years and the rest of the Pratt clan were informed around the time of Shari-Lea's pregnancy. The media claimed that the family had adopted a 'European' approach, whereby powerful men are almost always expected to have mistresses. Whatever the family's attitude to the situation, it was dealt with behind closed doors and all concerned appeared able to live with it. Pratt moved between his two families, safe in the knowledge that his profile was far lower in Sydney than in Melbourne, which gave him the relative freedom to live his life as he chose.

The situation changed once the media got a hold of the story, but the robust nature of the private company structure at Visy that kept the family united and working as one helped the family survive what was a major shock. The surprise was not so much the affair itself as the press's treatment of the story, as the private lives of Australian business leaders have traditionally been left alone by the mainstream press.

As a lifelong philanthropist and media-friendly businessman, Pratt did not expect a full-blown media exposé after *The Sydney Morning Herald* broke the story that he had another child outside the Pratt family. But he was wrong. The affair became a cause célèbre, especially in Sydney where minor characters in the story, including Julie Page, became overnight celebrities when they gave details about the affair to the media.

Exploiting the story for all it was worth, the tabloid press and current affairs shows competed with each other to dig up every possible detail concerning the Pratt family. For celebrity watchers, the story had everything—a billionaire, a younger woman, rambling mansions, private jets and family intrigue.

The news even spread beyond Australian borders. With one-third of Visy's operations located in the US, the New York–based business magazine *Forbes* had discovered the Pratt family and placed Richard Pratt on the Forbes 400 list of billionaires. In 2004 the magazine ranked Richard as the 356th-richest person on the planet. In 2002 the magazine commented not only on the success of Visy in the US, but also on Pratt's marital indiscretions.

In Australia the story of Richard and Shari-Lea certainly made headlines. The tabloids ran with it for all it was worth and the broadsheets also took part in the charge. Criticism of the media's decision to run the story erupted in parts of the business and Jewish communities and led to speculation as to the motivations and judgements of the broadsheets. *The Australian's* Jill Rowbotham wrote at length on the appropriateness or otherwise of publicly airing the issue, reporting that *Sydney Morning Herald* editor Paul McGough was undecided as to whether or not to publish the story until Ben Hills was inadvertently approached outside the courthouse.

Campbell Reid, editor of *The Australian*, likened the behaviour of *The Sydney Morning Herald* and *The Age* to a dog chasing a fire engine down the street and inadvertently catching it, claiming they had no idea what to do with the story the day after breaking it. Shelly Gare, in *The Australian* on 18 March, took a light-hearted view of the Shari-Lea issue, saying, 'If we are to bray in horror at Pratt's libidinous behaviour and deem it worthy of top-of-the-news coverage, why, let's be democratic and run a list of all notable Australian men with lovers on the side. It's only been going on since Caesar and Cleopatra. I gather it has something to do with the extra testosterone that goes with ambition. Or so they tell us.

'So let us take it for granted Pratt isn't Robinson Crusoe and think instead of the media melee's real casualty — the Hitchcock family dog that, said Thursday's *Daily Telegraph*, was skittled as Hitchcock's mother drove to her daughter's aid.'[4]

During the media frenzy, Channel Nine conducted an interview with Julie Page. Shari-Lea took court action to prevent the material going to air, and succeeded. At one stage during the Shari-Lea fiasco an insider who claimed to have knowledge of the affair tried to blackmail Pratt by demanding a $1.5 million payment in return for not going public with more information on the mistress matter.

The Pratt family culture of sticking together through thick and thin came to the fore when Jeanne Pratt released a statement pledging support for her husband. The couple chose to fly the flag of business (and relationship) as usual by attending an

official function to welcome Queen Elizabeth II and Prince
Philip to Melbourne at Government House. The two shook
hands with the royal couple while the nanny and the mistress
battled it out in a Sydney court. Richard Pratt beamed at the
Queen, resplendent in his navy suit. Jeanne, dressed in aqua,
was reportedly more reserved.

The Government House outing may have shown a commitment to continuing their old lifestyle, but in the months that
followed Pratt-watchers saw Richard change tack and make
a major withdrawal from public life. In late April 2000 he
stood down as Chancellor of Swinburne University; two
weeks later the family ceased their multimillion-dollar
support of sections of the arts, pledging instead to direct more
of their philanthropic efforts to areas of social need. Then,
in late May, Pratt resigned from the board of his beloved
Carlton Football Club, a position he had held since 1985,
saying he had decided to resign all directorships and public
office positions.[5]

It would appear that Shari-Lea felt no pressure to constrain
her public appearances and the tabloid press delighted in
reporting on her outings. On 22 April she was reported as
having been at the AJC Derby at Randwick racecourse in
Sydney in the company of John Sangster, internationally
renowned racehorse breeder and British football pools heir.
Later that year *The Daily Telegraph* spotted Shari-Lea at the
Melbourne Cup.

No doubt the media glare Pratt came under as a result of his
affair with Shari-Lea was painful and humiliating and took a
large toll. Speaking about it seven years on, he said, 'It's my
own business, it's my own problem with my own family. It is
of no interest—or shouldn't be of any interest—to anyone

else. But if the media want to talk about it, good luck to them. What can I do? I can't stop the media from doing whatever is legal, [but] some of it was very annoying'.[6]

His friends and supporters took a similar line. Trucking magnate Lindsay Fox simply pointed out that Richard and Jeanne had stayed together, something he saw as a credit to both of them. 'Jeanne is a marvellous lady. That "stand by your man" [attitude] was personified by the strength of Jeanne', Fox said. 'And Dick is entitled to run his life how he wants.' Long-time friend and Pratt Foundation Chief Executive Sam Lipski also saw the media coverage of the affair as an invasion of Pratt's privacy. 'To [Pratt] it was just the sheer injustice of it all. He never set himself up as some sort of moraliser, he wasn't a priest. So why was something which was entirely a matter for his own family to work out of interest to others, for no other reason than that he was a successful businessman?'[7]

His relationship with Shari-Lea spread another layer of complexity over the character of Richard Pratt, especially considering he had proclaimed so loudly that family was such an important part of his life. However, the nature of Pratt's relationship with Shari-Lea shows that in some senses he was not actually breaking his own dictums. Family remained important to him — the family had just grown, and Richard Pratt was never one to do things the way everyone else did.

Powerful men often have affairs or mistresses, but these are usually fly-by-night relationships where lovers are discarded or paid off into silence when they reach their use-by date. This was not the case for Richard Pratt. Shari-Lea and Paula remained permanent fixtures in his life, and Paula has even gained a level of acceptance from his first family.

If the Pratt family's acceptance of his relationship with Shari-Lea could be described as 'European', then so too could the relationship with Shari-Lea itself. Shari-Lea did not lead the traditional life of a mistress, waiting and pining until business affairs and family commitments finally afforded her lover the time for a rendezvous. Shari-Lea appears to have lived a full life throughout the time of her involvement with Pratt, with her name being linked to a range of other interesting men.

There was a sales manager with news agency Reuters (who is rumoured to have been given his marching orders by Pratt), Robert Sangster (with whom she shared the passion of owning racehorses) and Christopher Coon, an Englishman who dated actress Arkie Whiteley (daughter of painter Brett). Shari-Lea is also said to have had a friendship with a wealthy food retailer and entrepreneur, as well as property developer Sam Cahill, who had once been linked to former New South Wales Liberal leader Kerry Chikarovsky. Pratt apparently fretted over Shari-Lea's relationship with Cahill, thinking it was not good for his daughter or his mistress.[8]

Paula did not lack love or indulgence from her father as she grew up. Pratt would see her and her mother when he was in Sydney and the child enjoyed overseas holidays, often travelling in the Pratt family private jet. Jeanne is said to have developed a bond with the child who, incidentally, has the surname Hitchcock, not Pratt.

Pratt's relationship with Shari-Lea seems to have been a constant in his life, with Shari-Lea throwing regular parties with him when he visited Sydney. *The Sydney Morning Herald* reported that the last of these was thrown in celebration of his seventy-fourth birthday in December 2008, at his luxurious apartment at Circular Quay. He was ill with cancer at the time. Allan Hitchcock and Anthony Pratt were said to be in attendance, as were MP Frank Sartor and former Qantas chief Geoff Dixon. Bob Hawke and advertising guru John Singleton were also often on Pratt's Sydney guest list.

As his illness progressed, Pratt continued to maintain his relationship with his youngest daughter. He attended sports days, speech nights and open days at her school, and Shari-Lea told *The Sydney Morning Herald* that he travelled to Dapto, in Wollongong, in January 2009 to watch Paula ride in the show jumping competition. 'Richard went to great lengths to spend as much time as he could with Paula and he was always talking to her, trying to teach her as much as possible', she said. 'His face would light up when she entered the room. He would do anything for her.'[9]

Shari-Lea also reported that Pratt got angry when he could not see Paula as much because of her summer showjumping commitments. Even when his illness was at its worst he still went to watch her at Dapto, despite being in obvious pain.

Pratt's connection with Shari-Lea lasted right to the end. As Pratt lay dying, Jeanne allowed Shari-Lea to spend an hour with him at Raheen to say goodbye. The two women agreed it would be better if Shari-Lea did not attend the funeral; however, Paula flew down in the Visy private jet with her nanny to attend the funeral and say her final farewell to her doting father. Sam Lipski acknowledged her place in her father's life in his eulogy to the man he had become friends with sixty years earlier at University High School.

In death as in life Pratt provided for his second family. The Watsons Bay home and a sum of about $25 million were said to have been put in trust for Paula, to be managed by

Shari-Lea's father, Allan Hitchcock, until she comes of age. At the time of writing, details of any inheritance for Shari-Lea were unknown; however, neither Shari-Lea nor Paula will get a stake in Visy. As a point of comparison, Kerry Packer left his mistress, Julie Trethowan, more than $10 million, but the Packer family would not have her at his death bed or his funeral.

In August 2009 it was reported that Shari-Lea had expressed concern to her friends that lawyers had discovered Pratt had died without any assets in his own name. The assets apparently sit in a series of trusts whose beneficiaries are his first family. However, according to Pratt family insiders Richard's intention was to look after Paula financially and this will happen.

Visy will be held by Jeanne and her three children, who received an inheritance in their own rights of around $500 million in 2003 following the hiving off of Thorney, Pact and Pratt Industries.

Despite the wealth and social position her relationship with Richard afforded her, Shari-Lea is reported as saying that the situation had not been a bed of roses. On 1 June 2009 she told *The Sydney Morning Herald* that being constantly in the glare of media attention was inhumane. She felt exploited and judged and that people developed a false impression of her through the media. Shortly after Pratt's funeral she had to call the police to her home when a photographer leaned over the fence to get a picture of Paula while she was grieving.

But perhaps the final word in this saga should be left to Jeanne Pratt, the person with the most to juggle in living with the situation. Her comment on it was simple—'Put it this way: shit happens and life moves on.'[10]

Chapter 8

No shrinking violet

Many business leaders have nothing to say on the bigger issues facing society. They can only parrot the clichés about workers having to restrain wage claims or banks having to keep a lid on interest rates. New Zealand tycoon Graeme Hart, said to be the richest man in Australasia, who has had the courage to invest millions in underperforming companies that he believes can be turned around, is so averse to the public eye that at times he could not be persuaded to meet shareholders or even to attend his school reunion. Richard Pratt was different—he had an opinion on everything and he wanted everyone to know about it.

Pratt loved to take the stage. He loved to grab the microphone and tell the world what was on his mind. The performer in Pratt was never far from the surface—once he had an audience he wanted to win them over to his way of thinking. Not only did he talk, he often acted on what he said. Tackling striking workers with tough tactics is a public relations risk for any employer, but taking risks was what Richard Pratt did. In July 1999 hundreds of workers at Visy's Smithfield and Warwick Farm plants in Sydney held a stand-off with police when a nasty dispute hit the company after a protracted round of enterprise bargaining broke down. Delivery trucks were picketed and stopped from entering the plant. Visy brought in strikebreakers and there were some ugly confrontations between picketers and police.

The action by Visy clearly showed that what Pratt wanted to believe about his factories and what was actually happening on the factory floor did not always dovetail perfectly. By engaging Dr Stephen Webster, a consultant who later worked on the waterfront dispute with workplace minister Peter Reith, and former Patrick Corporation boss Chris Corrigan, Pratt showed he was prepared to fight tooth and nail with unions if he did not get his way on industrial relations.

Yet he was by no means 'anti-worker' and he maintained very strong relationships through all levels of his company, on the shop floor as well as with management. One man, Dante Bastiani, who spent five decades with Visy, was given a luxury car as a token of appreciation when he retired, and he visited his old boss at Raheen in his last days. Pratt boasted he had made many millionaires out of his employees and there was strong loyalty elicited on both sides of the relationship.

Living your life in the public eye means there will always be questions asked about your behaviour or your motives in any situation. A lifetime of public statements left Pratt open to plenty of contradictions. His tough tactics with the striking workers did little to convince sceptics working for the Visy group that it was any different to working for other companies. But Pratt's strong positions and statements should not be mistaken for personal or political inflexibility. His confrontations with the workers at the Smithfield and Warwick Farm plants, for example, do not paint him into a corner as an ideologue opposed to the union movement. Indeed, he also maintained friendships with people from within the labour movement and generally had good relations with his unionised workforce.

One such friendship was with Labor MP Bill Shorten, former Australian Workers Union chief and someone the smart money in the Labor Party views as a future prime minister. Shorten became close to Pratt after he married Pratt's goddaughter Debbie Beale. Debbie is the daughter of former Liberal MP and Visy director Julian Beale, and Jeanne Pratt is close to Julian's wife Felicity. The Pratt family hosted Bill and Debbie's engagement at Raheen and provided the mansion as a venue for fundraising events while Bill was head of the AWU. The two men did not always see eye to eye, but Richard was happy to vent their differences volubly and get on with life. Even when Bill and Debbie divorced in 2008 and Shorten began seeing Chloe Bryce, daughter of Governor-General Quentin Bryce, he remained friends with Pratt. Shorten was one of the many people who streamed to Dick Pratt's bedside in his final days and was visibly rocked by the prospect of his old friend's passing.

Pratt's motives on public issues were often questioned, particularly on schemes where Visy may directly profit such as recycling policies. While there may be something in those arguments, his stands were generally on issues that were far larger than his own personal interest. He believed that it was necessary to get involved whatever the price; whatever the complications it is better to act than not. Pratt's enduring contributions to debates on issues such as immigration, water conservation and Aboriginal reconciliation have helped change public consciousness on those issues.

Underlying his public policy activities was a deeply held belief that business has a role in the community to provide and enhance essential services. Pratt believed every business should engage with its community. On a micro level, a factory should engage with the locality it serves, and on a macro level the parent company should engage on national issues. At Visy, that meant Pratt was always keen to tell the government of the day how to manage the issues that affected his interests. This set him apart from most other industrialists. Reporters will seek the opinions of bankers and major exporters, but rarely 'box makers'. Ken MacKenzie, for example, Managing Director of Pratt's biggest local rival, Amcor, is rarely seen commenting on anything, including Amcor's future direction and operations.

To an extent the comparison is not a fair one. Chief executives of public companies represent their shareholders and as such cannot push their own political and social barrows without risking damage to the company's reputation or share price. But some have managed to get away with it, such as former Elders IXL/Foster's chief John Elliott and former Western Mining boss Hugh Morgan. And in 2008 Fortescue Metals Andrew 'Twiggy' Forrest launched a campaign to boost Indigenous employment by 50 000. Nonetheless, it is still easier for someone who owns the company to be outspoken and campaign on non-business issues. And yet, while there are a lot of private companies in Australia few of them are led by people who habitually raise their voices on issues not associated with their immediate business interests.

Richard Pratt's best known contribution to public debate had to do with the future direction of Australian water policy. His early days growing up on his parents' fruit block in Shepparton introduced him to water issues that city kids do not get the chance to learn about. The massive fruit industry that developed in the region is built on irrigation schemes. Pratt used to talk about his young days swimming in the irrigation channels and dams with his friend Digger James.

As drought became the norm across southern Australia from the late 1990s Pratt became concerned that the country's valuable water resources were being wasted. He typically thought big and came up with large-scale solutions. At first he proposed piping water down from the wet northern regions, but soon decided this was not a viable option. He then looked at the irrigation system and decided it was way below par in terms of water efficiency.

By 2002 Pratt had begun to view Australia's water situation as a national emergency, one that needed massive resources to be mobilised quickly to enable the country to come to grips with it. What he envisaged was a project that would rival the size and significance of the Snowy Mountain Scheme, which marshalled the water resources of the high country around Canberra from the 1940s to boost irrigation and create hydro-electricity. Pratt pledged that if governments took serious action, Visy would be prepared to invest $100 million of its own funds. 'I'm sixty-eight years old. I want to do something for Australia before I go and I'd like to be involved in this water thing', Pratt said at the time.[1]

In 2003 Visy, along with the federal and New South Wales governments, launched a $5.3 million study of the efficiency of the Murrumbidgee Valley irrigation system, which came up with some startling findings. There was some 1.3 million megalitres of water unaccounted for in the system each year. There was scope to invest $824 million on water-saving technologies in the region and this would bring a return of $293 million in increased farm production each year. So on a national level the investment would be paid off in less than three years. This gave Pratt further confidence that the economics of water investment could stack up.

But it was the centre point of his water vision that got people talking. Pratt said that much of Australia's open irrigation ditches should be put into pipes—pipes made from recycled plastic and, of course, Visy would benefit as it was in the recycled plastics business. Some of the largest dams in the country also needed covering with plastic, he argued.

Piping the irrigation system would save up to thirty per cent of the water that currently evaporates or leaks out of channels. The Pratt proposal was for government to issue water bonds that would entice private investors, such as superannuation funds, to invest for returns of six per cent to seven per cent a year. His system would have used pipes of between ten centimetres and 100 centimetres in diameter, and where possible they could piggyback on existing infrastructure such as gas pipelines or railway lines.

Pratt explained his thinking on water efficiency to the Wealth from Water conference at Wagga Wagga in March 2003. 'All the water in the cities is sold at whatever price the authorities decide to sell it at, and ninety-nine per cent of it is invoiced', he said. 'What I'm saying is, the agricultural world uses seventy-five per cent of all the water that's used in Australia, and yet only fifty per cent of what they let out of their reservoirs is invoiced. So what the tenet is, don't waste the other fifty per cent. Now that's a simple tenet. That wasn't where I started. Where I started was I had a dream of bringing the monsoon rainwater down from the north to the south, but I was told very firmly by those interested in our environment that that's not on.

'Now in the deserts of the Middle East, [with their] flash floods, they're now identifying how to capture that water. And this was known to the Assyrians 5000 years ago, but we've lost it. We've got to capture every bit of water as it falls and use it to the best advantage of the people instead of letting it flow out to the sea.'[2]

When asked whether his proposals were just money-making ventures for Visy he replied, 'In the long term it's about everybody making a lot more money. It's about Australia being richer, leaving something behind when I fall off the twig. It's one of those things that everybody when he gets to sixty-eight thinks about. But if they're rich enough and they've got their head screwed on right, they do something more than think about it'.

It was classic Pratt—broadcasting his opinions to the widest possible audience. He made no excuses: he ran a business and he wanted that business to succeed. But, crucially, Pratt linked that desire for success with a rational desire for a better Australia. There might have been contradictions in this approach, but Pratt has helped people, from boardroom executives to workers in logging towns, understand that community and business can have mutual goals.

He took a practical approach to providing the $100 million for his water vision. Pratt Water, a company he set up in 2003, signed a deal with ANZ Bank in early 2004 that committed the company to providing $10 million a year for ten years to finance water efficiency measures taken by the private sector in irrigation areas. 'I have long believed that many Australian farmers know the benefits of switching to high-technology irrigation, which can result in water savings of fifty per cent and more', he said. 'But often they lack the funds or the confidence to proceed. If we can work with a major bank like ANZ to enhance the credit status of farmers wanting to make the switch, we can achieve real water savings. If this model proves successful the federal government should consider providing funds for farmers to make on-farm water savings with the saved water going back to our rivers.'[3]

In the end, however, Pratt's water vision ultimately came to nothing. He could not get the government support he wanted and the private sector did not want to invest in it either. In October 2006 a Visy spokesman told *The Age* Pratt was disillusioned and had walked away from his water commitment.

Despite the result, the water campaign was not simply hype. Pratt invested over $5 million in a public campaign over the four years he pushed the water strategy, and undoubtedly his commitments helped to raise awareness of the water issue. Had the plan taken off, no doubt Visy would have profited from selling recycled plastic pipes, but the country would have boosted its water resources and agricultural output. Perhaps Pratt's proposal was simply too early or he was too optimistic about what could be realistically achieved. Action in this area has started, if slowly, with the Victorian Government commencing the Wimmera Mallee pipeline project in late 2006, which will eventually see the rollout of thousands of kilometres of plastic irrigation pipe.

Trying to avoid criticism as a politically engaged billionaire would be like trying to score in a footy match without making contact with another player. Richard waded into most debates with his eyes open and his fists raised. He proudly took top prize in environmental awards—in September 1998 he was named Environmental Visionary of the Year by the Keep Australia Beautiful campaign—despite some environmentalists claiming he was simply a link in a longer chain of environmental degradation. But from the Pratt point of view, the paper industry must exist and Visy's approach is to be the best in the business. A corporate governance survey released in October 2003 from Reputex Australia named Visy as the best performer in terms of conservation policy among the top 200 Australian companies.

Entering key debates in a public and creative manner, Richard Pratt was always in the news, and the bulk of the reportage reflected well on him and the company he ran. Moreover, inside Visy it reminded employees Visy was not just another company. His reputation for 'making a difference' represents a lifetime of work for a business leader who had strong opinions about how society could be better organised.

Other highly controversial stances Pratt took related to Australia's population and immigration policy. He, along with a number of other businessmen and former prime minister Malcolm Fraser, advocated a major immigration increase that would see Australia's population reach fifty million by

2050. Their argument was that greater immigration was the key not only to Australia's economic survival, but its national security. Many environmentalists disagreed, concerned that the country was already approaching, or indeed may have passed, its optimal sustainable population. Scientist Tim Flannery in his iconic book *The Future Eaters* suggested a sustainable population for Australia may be as small as ten million, while former Australia Institute executive director Clive Hamilton has said immigration should be cut and a total population target of twenty-two million should be aimed for.

Pratt saw the issue differently. At the launch of lobby group The Australian Population Institute in November 1999 he called on the nation to 'pursue a vision which looks ahead fifty years to a democratic, secure, prosperous, fair and pluralist Australia with a population of fifty million people'. He argued that with Australia's population set to stabilise at around twenty-three million by 2025, and twenty-five per cent of that figure to be aged over sixty-five, planning for population growth was the most crucial issue the country faced.

At one stage Pratt advocated doubling both the immigration and the refugee intakes to increase the population by around 200 000 a year, arguing that Australia's low level of immigration was 'ultimately indefensible in the international community'.[4] He saw no contradiction in this and his concern for Australia's dwindling water reserves. It was not that the country did not have enough water, he argued, it was just that we were wasting a large amount of what we had.

While not afraid to be outspoken on public policy Pratt did not get into personal slanging matches with politicians. He remained on good terms with former prime minister John

Howard, although he strongly disagreed with Howard's stance on refugees, favouring a less punitive policy. He was also critical of Howard's refusal to come out strongly against Pauline Hanson's One Nation party and her anti-immigration stance in the late 1990s, and he put these views strongly to Howard in private. In a speech at Raheen in 1998 marking the fiftieth anniversary of Visy, Richard spoke at length about his family history, stressing how Australia had long offered refuge to those escaping oppression elsewhere and how the country had benefited from immigration. Though Howard, Hanson and One Nation were never mentioned the message was clear.

While delivering the Australia Day address in Sydney in 2005 Pratt said, 'The waves of immigration which transformed Australia for the better in the twentieth century have to be renewed if we're to compete and prosper in the twenty-first century'. He also listed a number of what he termed his commandments, which included: improved water management and distribution; signing the Kyoto Protocol; increased spending on research and development; the use of some Treasury savings bonds as education bonds to offset the rising costs of tertiary education; tax rebates for companies that donate a percentage of profits to community groups, to encourage more companies to do so; and an 'Australia Plan' to support young Australian volunteers to engage in South-East Asia. Some of those, particularly his advocacy of signing the Kyoto Protocol, the measures to boost corporate philanthropy and the call for increased research spending, would have stuck in a few craws in government and business at the time.

In the same speech he challenged what was then the widely accepted economic orthodoxy that government should run surpluses, and debt was just for the private sector. 'The time has come to take on new debt to help secure our nation's future', he said. 'Debt is good. At least the right kind of debt is good. The financial markets, Treasury officials and the economists are all very capable of distinguishing between unproductive debt and wealth-generating debt that builds national infrastructure and pays for itself through job creation and economic stimulation.'[5] He went on to argue that on almost any international comparison, Australia lagged behind on infrastructure spending. That might sound unremarkable now, but prior to the global financial crisis such statements would have been particularly provocative in business, bureaucratic and financial circles.

Former New South Wales premier Bob Carr, the man charged with choosing the Australia Day speaker, had a year earlier given some inadvertent support to Pratt's position on refugees when he wrote that Australia should have taken in more refugees in the late 1930s: 'Imagine how Australia would have taken off after 1945 with a dozen Frank Lowys or Dick Pratts—inventions, industries and orchestras'.[6]

Pratt's tendency to make his opinions heard ensured he did not fit easily into the often grey world of corporate life. His relationship with the business elite who run Australia—in particular with the Melbourne establishment—was complex. For all his fame and fortune in business circles, Richard was invited to join few corporate boards. Certainly his regular outbursts against the ineptitude and greed of Australia's largest corporations indicated he was keeping his eye on the nation's elite, but many among them would have been most uncomfortable having such a single-minded over achiever on their team.

Breaking new ground for business leaders, Richard Pratt also openly clashed with government policy on the issue of Aboriginal reconciliation. Famously, Pratt publicly disagreed with John Howard's refusal to apologise over the Stolen Generations, commenting, 'I see no particular problem with apologising for what others might have done out of ignorance and bad behaviour on their part'.[7] Using his influence and money to push Australian society in the direction he believed was best for the country, Pratt invested, literally, in Aboriginal reconciliation through his support for Pat Dodson. A senior Aboriginal leader and former chairman of the Council for Aboriginal Reconciliation, Dodson had a public spat with John Howard in 1997 over a number of issues, including native title.

For a time, Dodson found himself outside the circle of influence in Canberra that determines Aboriginal policy. Pratt admired his work though, and through an organisation he chaired called the Australia Foundation for Culture and Humanities, later rebranded the Australian Business Arts Foundation (ABAF), funded the Australian Indigenous Cultural Network in 1998, which Dodson chaired.

Striding the public stage and offering informed opinion on government policy worked well for Richard Pratt over the years, but he was much too pragmatic a businessman to ever believe trends in the wider economy would determine the future of his company. In other words, though he constantly sought 'big picture' improvements through provocative work in philanthropy, in business the Cardboard King just got on with the job.

Chapter 9

True blue Aussie

The European migrants who left their homelands for Australia during the twentieth century, fleeing war or oppression, or simply seeking a better life, were quick to embrace the culture and lifestyle of their new country. They adopted beach holidays and homeownership, but were not prepared to give up everything they held dear. Soccer was one of those reminders of the old country that afforded an outlet for generations of European migrants, enriching the sporting culture of their new country in the process.

Before soccer went national and non-ethnic in 2005 with the formation of the Football Federation Australia and the A-League, the old state-based leagues reflected the ethnic loyalties of Europe — South Melbourne Hellas for the Greeks,

Juventus for the Italians, Essendon Croatia for the Croats. In Sydney Jewish immigrants followed this trend, supporting the Hakoah soccer club, but the Jews who settled in Melbourne did something different. They eschewed the round ball game they knew so well and flocked to Aussie Rules. While not many Jews have ever actually made it to the top level of the sport, the Jewish immigrant community's football passions have been directed largely towards the Carlton Football Club.

This was not necessarily so of the established Anglo-Jewish community, which lived south of the Yarra River. But the Eastern European migrants of the twentieth century often settled in Carlton and the inner-north when they arrived, and so they followed the local football team. Today it is estimated that twenty-five per cent of Melbourne's 60 000 or so Jews support Carlton.

Not that the club was predominantly Jewish. Its players and supporters come from all backgrounds and it has had significant support from the Italian community, which called the suburb of Carlton home for many decades. High-profile blue-blood Carlton supporters have included long-serving prime minister Sir Robert Menzies, who would view games from his chauffeur-driven Bentley, and another Liberal former prime minister, Malcolm Fraser.

For Richard Pratt in particular, football played a huge part in his induction into Australian life. In Shepparton Richard's friend Digger James taught him how to swim in the irrigation channels, how to speak English and the intricacies of the local football code. That started what for Richard became a lifelong obsession with the game of football. He played school football and at sixteen, when the family moved to Melbourne, he became a keen footballer for University High School.

University High is located in Parkville, which is adjacent to Carlton, so Richard, like so many other Jewish kids had before him, adopted the religion of Carlton Football Club. In 1952, his matriculation year, he was made a prefect and played in the ruck for the University High firsts.

The firsts were quite a team. The captain at the time was Allen Aylett, who later captained North Melbourne. His fellow players described Pratt as big and solid, with the biggest chest in the team. He had a booming voice and liked to show off his strength by bending beer bottle tops between his thumb and forefinger. But Pratt was more a strong player than a rough one. 'He stood up for himself and his style was to get out there and go through with things. He was big and people got out of his way, but he wasn't punchy', a former teammate said.

Pratt liked his football so much that while he was at school he also pulled on boots for the Carlton under 19s. In 1951, his first year with the Blues, he won the club's most consistent player award. The following year Pratt began studying commerce at Melbourne University, but remained serious about his football. Rather than join one of the amateur clubs at the university, he maintained his association with Carlton by playing again in the under 19 and reserve grade teams. He was so successful in his first year with the club that he won the Morrish Medal for the best and fairest player in the Victorian Football League's under 19s competition.

But football had to compete with other things in Richard Pratt's busy life. There were his studies at university, working in the family business and a burgeoning acting career which began at Melbourne University. He soon dropped out of university, travelled overseas as an actor and eventually ended the first part of his formal association with Carlton after five seasons in the reserves and under 19s teams.

However, when Pratt returned from his international pursuits he took up football again. In 1957 the Jewish community's amateur football team, AJAX, had joined the Victorian Amateur Football Association competition for the first time. A year later, when Pratt returned from overseas, he donned its red, white and black colours and took the field for the club. His style was somewhat unusual to say the least. Eyewitnesses report that after kicking a goal Pratt would burst into song, using his by now well-trained baritone. He would also instruct his rover in Yiddish, an amalgam of German, Hebrew and the Slavic languages, and the lingua franca of the Pratt household when Richard was growing up.

Even after Pratt had made it big in business he remained a consistent contributor to Carlton in terms of donations and sponsorship. He served on the board from 1985 to 2000 (resigning shortly after news of his extramarital affair emerged) and employed a number of current and former footballers at Visy. These included Keith McKenzie, a former North Melbourne coach who also had an association with Carlton. McKenzie has worked for Visy's human resources department for twenty-five years. Current Carlton president and long-time club captain Stephen 'Sticks' Kernahan left stockbroking in the recession of the 1990s and worked for Visy for a couple of years before starting his own printing business, Docklands Press. Kernahan says he learned a lot during his time at Visy.

Even during the early years Pratt always made his presence felt at Carlton. During one famous incident, Pratt was drinking with former Carlton ruckman Percy Jones, then a fellow board member, when they began discussing Israel. Pratt strongly defended the country's leadership and scorned Australia's treatment of Aborigines. Jones retorted, 'At least we didn't send in the army like you did to the Palestinians'.

Pratt took the remark to be anti-Semitic, things heated up and the two men stepped outside. 'What I meant was that we should go outside and talk about it, but he obviously thought I'd invited him out for a fight', Jones recalls. '[Pratt] threw a punch at me and hit me right on the nose. He didn't break it but he left a cut.'[1] Jones says he tried to slap Pratt back, but his swing missed. The following Monday the two men made up.

His time on the Carlton board during the 1980s kept Pratt in close contact with long-time Carlton president John Elliott. The two had a history, as Elliott had led the Elders group, once the epitome of Australia's conservative rural industries, on a buying spree that included Carlton and United Breweries in 1983. The breweries were major users of cardboard for their beer boxes, so Visy and Elders had done a great deal of business together.

Some of that business involved more than just beer boxes, and caught the eye of regulators. In the 1980s corporate Australia caught the takeover bug that was raging through Wall Street, and former industrial icons such as breweries and manufacturing firms were bought by a new breed of corporate raiders. The process reached a crescendo mid decade with a series of bids by smooth-talking Western Australian trader Robert Holmes à Court to buy what was then the country's biggest company, BHP. The first bid, made through a small Western Australian bulldozer dealer named Wigmores, was no more than nuisance value. But in 1986, Holmes à Court tried again. By the time of his last bid Wigmores had morphed into a major company, Bell Resources, and BHP's supporters in the corporate world were worried.

Then at the last moment BHP was put out of Holmes à Court's reach when Elders IXL, with John Elliott as its chief, bought twenty per cent of BHP for $2 billion, and BHP bought $1 billion worth of Elders preference shares. At the same time, Pratt and New Zealand businessman Allan Hawkins bought a crucial 4.4 per cent stake in BHP through a New South Wales registered company for $506 million. The deal was seen by the market as Pratt's way of helping Elliott keep Holmes à Court at bay by denying him a stake that would have been useful in his BHP campaign.

The episode triggered a National Crime Authority (NCA) investigation, focusing on a series of very complicated deals. Pratt's office was raided, documents were taken and he likened the investigation to living in a state controlled by the Nazis.[2] A lot of mud was thrown and a parliamentary inquiry heard the NCA had evidence that Elliott had organised a $52 million purchase of shares in a Pratt company. In July 1994 Pratt and Elliott were both sued by Foster's over this share transaction, but the court never ruled on an outcome. It is believed the matter was resolved out of court.

In 1986 Ray Shoer, the executive director of the National Companies and Securities Commission (a forerunner of the Australian Securities & Investments Commission), did serious damage to Pratt's public image when he questioned Pratt's reputation in the Victorian Supreme Court. (The NCSC was examining events around a takeover bid for glass packaging group ACI, where Pratt and Allan Hawkins and his New

Zealand–based Equitycorp group had been acting as partners in a bid for the company.)

Stunning the courtroom Shoer told the court, 'The problem was that further investigation had increased the Commission's concerns, not of the honesty of Equiticorp, but of the conduct of the Pratt group'. Shoer also told the court, 'The Commission was more concerned that Mr Pratt's undertaking might not have the same value as the one given by Mr Hawkins'.[3]

Hawkins was charged with fraud by the Serious Fraud Office in New Zealand and subsequently jailed over transactions relating to shares in BHP and ACI. No charges were ever laid against Pratt and his employees and all documents that had been seized were eventually returned. A separate case against Elliott and some of his executives eventually collapsed when a Victorian supreme court judge found that the NCA had acted outside its terms of reference. This ruling was later overturned but under Victorian law the case could not be reheard. Then Pratt lieutenant Michael Naphtali said Pratt had developed a 'real sense of injustice and inequity' over the NCA investigation and cited it as one of the main reasons the tycoon chose to grow his business so large in the US.

John Elliott was a larger than life figure in the 1980s. His corporate raiding put him in control of one of the largest industrial companies in the country and he set off to 'Fosterise the world' by buying an international beer empire. His personal fortune was said to be worth $80 million at its peak. From 1987 to 1990 Elliott was national president of the Liberal Party and was widely touted as a future prime minister. From 1983 to 2002 he served as president of the Carlton Football Club.

Carlton, as its team colours suggest, is Aussie rules blue blood and as old as the game of football itself. The club was formed in 1864 and won its first official premiership in 1871. In the postwar years the Blues lagged somewhat, spending most of the 1950s out of the final four. Their fortunes started to change when the legendary Ron Barassi came over from Melbourne in 1965, serving as captain coach for a few years before handing on-field control over to man mountain John Nicholls. By 1967 the Blues were back in the final four and went on to win the premiership flag in 1968 and 1970.

From then until the late 1980s, the Blues were a dynamo, winning seven premierships between 1968 and 1987 under the on-field leadership of men such as the dazzlingly brilliant Alex 'Jezza' Jesaulenko, towering ruckman and now noted financier Mike Fitzpatrick and another tall man, Stephen 'Sticks' Kernahan. In the early days of his presidency Big John, as he was called, created electricity around the club with his booming voice and 'stuff you' attitude to authority and convention. In 1995 the Blues won another flag, were runners up in 1999 and Big John's mates in the money world were opening their wallets to the club.

But as the new decade dawned things started to go pear-shaped for Carlton. The greats such as Sticks and Fitzpatrick, Jezza and full-back Steven Silvagni, who like his father Sergio before him had shone for years at Carlton, were gone or were going. Finding replacements was hard and the club moved into the doldrums. During Big John's presidency Carlton tried to buy success, flagrantly breaching the salary cap regulations, which were part of the 'sporting socialism' regime run by the AFL to keep the competition as even as possible.

In October 2000 Carlton was fined $100 000 for breaches of its salary cap back in 1998. Media commentators, ever keen to give Big John a bit of his own medicine, attacked his earlier stance against Essendon as hypocritical. The previous year Essendon had been fined $250 000 for salary cap breaches and Elliott had called them cheats. He even claimed that since the offences occurred in 1993, the year Essendon defeated Carlton in the grand final, Essendon should be stripped of the premiership so it could be given to the Blues.

Elliott also pushed his trademark brand free market economics, which he advocated for so strongly in politics, into the football arena. He wanted Carlton to be able to deal with its own media rights and had some success in the area. The commentators accused him of plotting to abolish the salary cap and player draft system, something they said would split the league into rich and poor, leaving the competition as uneven as English soccer where a few clubs constantly dominate the premiership tables.

By now the Elliott years were drawing to a close. What once had been the cocky arrogance of a man who did not mind rocking the boat had morphed into a caricature of himself. The year 2000 was mixed for the Carlton president. He was forced to write a letter of apology after behaving inappropriately at the AFL Players' Association annual awards night. However, he also took the AFL and Channel Seven to court over ground access and internet issues and won.[4] But Big John's star was waning. *The Australian*'s outspoken football writer, Patrick Smith, wrote at the time, 'Such is Elliott's aggressive and buoyant nature he will brush off this latest catastrophe [the $100 000 fine for breaching the salary cap] as a hiccup, but even by his standard it is a loud one. His significance as a major player in AFL affairs continues to be diminished'.[5]

By the end of 2002 there was mutiny in the ranks at the Blues. Former Carlton chief executive and Docklands Stadium boss Ian Collins claimed that Big John was deluded and challenged Elliott for the presidency with a group of backers known as Carlton One. Elliott tried legal action to prevent the challenge, but ultimately fell on his sword. The papers were full of his epitaphs in November, such as the following:

'His greatest achievements in two decades of football admin-istration would be overseeing the introduction of the AFL Commission and the national competition and retaining Carlton's leasehold on Optus Oval as a future bargaining chip and generator of revenue.

'Judged in the harsh light of day, however, the legacy Elliott bequeaths to Carlton and Ian Collins' new board is mixed at best. Elliott's role in revamping the nature of corporate sponsorship and recruitment in the 1980s should not be ignored, nor the two premierships that came Carlton's way under his twenty-year reign. If footballers are judged on their last game then Elliott should be judged on the shape in which he leaves Carlton. A dismal tally of two wins for the year was as much a product of Elliott's short-sighted view of recruiting as it was bad luck or injuries.'[6]

A few days later, the AFL laid further charges of salary cap rorting against Carlton. In late November the club was hit with a $930 000 fine and lost priority picks in the AFL draft for two years. That meant it lost the right to recruit four of the best young players in the competition and its prospects for an on-field recovery were thwarted completely. In late

2002 Carlton announced it had an annual loss for the year of $7.5 million. The Elliott legacy would be felt for years to come.

John Elliott remained a figure of controversy after leaving the Carlton presidency. In 2005 he declared himself bankrupt following the collapse of his rice milling company, Water Wheel Holdings, which was found to have traded while insolvent. Richard Pratt had supported his old mate in this venture having bought 5.4 per cent of Water Wheel in 1998.

At the time of writing Water Wheel was scheduled to rise from the ashes as the owner of a large gypsum deposit in Shandong province in China with Elliott family interests as minor shareholders following a corporate restructure. He hit the headlines again in mid 2009 by claiming that Carlton had paid off women who he claimed alleged they had been sexually assaulted by Carlton players.

Under the new leadership of Ian Collins, Carlton was forced to deal with rising costs as the bill for the building of the Legends grandstand blew out to over $20 million. Collins was a well-liked character at the club and seen as a professional; however, during his reign Carlton continued to linger at the bottom of the ladder. After finishing as wooden spooners in Elliott's last year of presidency, Carlton's record reads fifteenth (in a sixteen-side competition), eleventh and two more wooden spoons before Ian Collins decided to call it quits and handed the presidency to Graham Smorgon in 2006.

Smorgon, a commercial lawyer and entrepreneur, came from classic Jewish Carlton pedigree. His family migrated from Russia in the 1920s and developed a massive private industrial operation that included meat, paper, steel and plastics. His cousin David was president of Western Bulldogs, a connection that was built up over generations because the Smorgon industrial business was not far from the Bulldogs Western Oval home.

Graham Smorgon put in a big effort at Carlton with observers saying he devoted endless time and expertise to the club. But a footy club lives and dies by its on-field performance and Carlton was still scraping the bottom of the barrel. In 2006 Carlton again received the wooden spoon and the club was not a happy place. 'People too took great pleasure in seeing Carlton where they were and the press had a field day', recalls current Carlton President Stephen Kernahan. 'We just had to cop it.'

Supporters were disheartened and there was dissent on the board with insiders complaining people within the club were leaking information to the media. What was discussed one day would appear in the newspapers the next. The club was also slipping financially as on-field performance dived and support waned. Smaller crowds at the games meant lower gate receipts and lower membership receipts as members became dispirited and left the club.

Several Carlton heavy hitters also became disaffected, with board members John Valmorbida and Bruce Mathieson walking out the door. Both were wealthy businessmen and spoke for the kind of money and community clout Carlton could not afford to lose.

In early 2007 board elections were held and it was clear to many that it was time for a change. Smorgon lost his seat along with art dealer Lauraine Diggins and Marcus Rose. In their place were businessman Paul Littmann, barrister Marcus Clark (son of runner Ron) and canny political operator Ari Suss. Suss had run two successful election campaigns for then Victorian Labor premier Steve Bracks and was the first real political nous on the Carlton board for some years. At the end of January, a new board with twelve members was in place but they were lacking a leader. Stephen Kernahan, who had been on the board since 1997, took on the role of interim president, but he was not interested in the job for himself.

What happened next is a matter of some conjecture, with various parties claiming credit for bringing Pratt to Carlton. In a nutshell, John Elliott approached Pratt, setting up a meeting. At the meeting Elliott, Kernahan, and former players Wes Lofts and Adrian Gleeson explained the position of the club to Pratt and told him it needed leadership. Pratt's response to their call for help was to volunteer for the presidency.

Of course the deal had to be approved by the full club board, which happened in an instant. Pratt put only one condition on his offer: his appointment was to be announced a week after their first meeting and if news of it leaked beforehand the deal was off. The board remained tight-lipped and no media got hold of the story before the official announcement. 'When Dick became president, it was as if everyone at Carlton had come out of the hailstorm and into the sunshine', Kernahan later recalled. 'That's how we all felt.'[7]

Pratt embraced the job of fixing Carlton with passion and power and set the scene for a strong, if somewhat autocratic, leadership style. He told the board that the club rooms needed to be refurbished to ensure the environment had a winning feel. They were thinking of perhaps paying off the $8 million in debt the club was carrying, but Pratt had other ideas. To make it clear that his commitment to the club was absolute and ease their concerns he paid for the refurbishment out of his own pocket.

Pratt also introduced a sense of informality right from his first board meeting. Those in attendance say that everyone was seated Pratt looked around the table and boomed, 'I thought this was a football club!' 'It is', someone replied. 'Well then where's the fucking beer?' Pratt demanded. The situation was quickly put right and Pratt's unique leadership style was asserted.

Next, Pratt met with club employees who were demoralised and fearing for their jobs given the pessimism that had overtaken Carlton in recent times. He met AFL executives and club supporters. To everyone he met Pratt gave out the same message: Carlton no longer has money problems. He was there to back the club and would make sure there was enough money to drive its success.

Pratt immediately turned his mind to staffing, believing that the club needed to employ the best people in order to succeed. He got out his chequebook and hired Rod Ashman, former Blues player and teacher, to mentor the players, and boosted PR and finance efforts with new appointments. But Pratt also had his eyes on a bigger prize—he wanted to appoint a new CEO. He had a look around and decided there were two main contenders: Brian Cook from Geelong and Greg Swann from Collingwood. It has been said that Pratt was reluctant to poach Cook from Geelong president, long-time friend and Visy box customer Frank Costa, so he approached

Swann, instead. A week later, Swann agreed to come over to Carlton.

In 2007 Carlton won the preseason NAB Cup competition. Pratt threw a fundraiser that brought in $2 million and in early April Carlton pulled off a convincing seventeen point win over Melbourne to start the season on a positive note. While debt was still a worry for the club, Pratt was thinking more about the long term. His idea was to try to raise money to get the team up and going so the club would rise with it.

Richard Pratt was a big presence in the Carlton boardroom and some say that he ran it like he owned it. Paul Littmann agrees that he was a strong figure. 'He was always there, one of the first to meetings, and he ran them', Littmann recalls. 'He was overly aggressive at times and dominant. He'd bite people's heads off.

'People weren't really scared of him. Everyone was there of their own volition for no financial rewards, and no-one went in assuming he'd be there, so no-one went there to be on his coat-tails. But we were in favour of him as president because of his enormous wealth. On a personal basis people might get upset because he said this or that, but in the main everyone thought we were heading in the right direction. There were no great controversies.

'He had a restless impatience that wanted to see the club's fortunes pick up quicker than they did. He also had a businessman's dislike of bureaucratic obstacles. When it came to sourcing new talent, he'd ask who the best player in the league in the position in question was. Then he'd say, "Well, let's just buy him". We'd say, "Dick, you can't buy [players] any more. It doesn't work like that". He'd adhere to it when he understood and never said, "Let's find a way around this".'

Pratt also possessed another attribute board members liked: he wanted meetings over quickly. Under his control board meetings rarely lasted longer than an hour, whereas under some of his predecessors they had stretched as long as five hours.

There was a magnetic quality about Richard Pratt. His enthusiasm, along with his money, made a big difference to the club. The Pratts also opened the doors of their mansion, Raheen, to players and club officials for countless bonding and fundraising events. At one such event Jeanne Pratt addressed players on the story of her redevelopment of Raheen. Thinking they would be bored Richard signalled her to finish up. She said if anyone wanted to know more she would be happy to talk to them later. An observer was surprised at the number of players lining up to speak to her.

Pratt was also a kind of one-man marketing machine. He attended most games while he was healthy and was a regular speaker at pre-game lunches. Numbers at these events would jump from 250 to 500, 'because people wanted to say they had lunch with Dick Pratt', says Littman.

Carlton players and officials liked the glamour of the Pratt lifestyle. Trips in the $50 million private jet, complete with discussions and planning sessions with Pratt, impromptu lunches at fashionable eateries, as well as access to business and cultural leaders. At Pratt's memorial service in Melbourne's Hamer Hall, AFL boss Andrew Demetriou recounted a story of Pratt holding up his private jet in Brisbane to wait for a giant tub of Kentucky Fried Chicken to be delivered after Carlton was given a 117-point trouncing by the Brisbane Lions. It might be an endearing story, but flying back to Melbourne there was some tough decision-making. After Pratt and his officials returned to Melbourne, coach Dennis Pagan was given his marching orders in favour of his understudy Brett Ratten. Former captain Anthony Koutoufides retired eight days later.

Pratt got a buzz from hanging out with the players and his friendship with wild forward-line star Brendan 'Fev' Fevola was well known. '[Pratt] idolised the players ... they were doing what he always wanted to do as a kid — playing senior football for Carlton', says Littman. 'Being president, winning the Morrish medal in the thirds is all okay, but running out in front of 100 000 people and kicking the winning goal in the grand final is every Melbourne boy's dream. He was still like a little boy with them. It wasn't, "Do what I tell you Fev", it was, "Let's have a drink Fev".'

Unfortunately, Pratt's money and magic did not have a supernatural effect on Carlton. During the first year of his presidency the club managed to move up only one rung from wooden spooners to fifteenth on the ladder, with four wins compared to three in 2006.

The highest profile coup in the Pratt era was the recruitment of West Coast captain and Brownlow and Norm Smith medallist Chris Judd at the end of the 2007 season. Judd had made it known that he was through with West Coast after six years and a premiership victory as captain, and that he wanted to play in his hometown of Melbourne. Judd was hot football property and four clubs tried to win him over — Collingwood, Melbourne, Carlton and Essendon.

Being out of contract Judd put himself forward to be traded. Such was his attractiveness as a player that he interviewed the four clubs who wanted him and made the decision on where to play himself. After being wooed by all four clubs and reportedly being offered the captaincy by Pratt, Judd eventually chose Carlton. But Carlton needed to do some fancy footwork to make sure that West Coast were well compensated for losing their star, a stipulation Judd had made during negotiations.

Eventually, Carlton worked out an arrangement with West Coast to give the Perth club its number three and number twenty draft selections, along with young footballer Josh Kennedy. After Judd and West Coast agreed to the deal Carlton Chief Executive Greg Swann said he was unsure what had finally swung Judd to pick Carlton. 'But we sold him on [the potential of] our young list … We told him that we had a stable board and administration and we went over the plans for our new facilities', Swann recalls. '[Coach] Brett Ratten and Chris had a long chat and we basically outlined our vision for the club and where we think we're at.'[8]

It was speculated that Carlton would pay Judd $1 million to play for them, money that was available without breaching the salary cap. Judd became the Blues' captain in 2008 and now also works for Visy as a company ambassador. Winning Judd's services was a major achievement for Carlton and many believed it was Pratt's magnetism together with his enthusiasm for the club and the money to back it up that finally swung the balance in their favour.

Pratt was also influential in another move the club hoped would have a long-term effect—building the new state-of-the-art training facility at Princes (now Visy) Park. Under Pratt's leadership the club planned to build an elite training facility that would include a gymnasium, running tracks and hot and cold water training tubs. The local population was to be accommodated with community facilities including meeting rooms and lecture theatres. Support was received from the state government and local council allowing the $12 million stage one of the project to begin. Current Carlton President Stephen Kernahan says the club decided it would be cheaper to do the project all at once and has therefore committed to the $17.5 million stage two development.

Ultimately, Richard Pratt's return to Carlton was short-lived. In December 2005, long before he took up the presidency, the Australian Competition and Consumer Commission (ACCC) launched proceedings against Visy, Richard Pratt and two of his executives over price-fixing arrangements with competitor Amcor, which had come to light the previous year. At first, Pratt denied his involvement, but on 8 October 2007, less than a week after Chris Judd was signed, Pratt reached a commercial settlement with the ACCC admitting his involvement and incurring a $36 million fine in the process.

This was a major blow to Pratt's reputation and did not look good for Carlton, either. There was negative commentary in the media. In early November Carlton declared its support for its president with CEO Greg Swann saying that AFL chief Andrew Demetriou had not indicated that the league had any concerns about Pratt's tenure.

However, the media did not let up, with *The Australian*'s Patrick Smith referring to Pratt as 'The Price-Fixer'. By late March 2008, there was more heat on Pratt with news being leaked that Demetriou had been questioned by members of the AFL Players Association at a conference in late 2007 as to why the league had not pushed for Pratt to stand down when the price-fixing scandal was brought to light.

Then, in mid April, Pratt himself came out and asked the AFL to put its support behind him. 'Not one member of the AFL Commission or administration has contacted either me or any official of Carlton questioning my tenure', Pratt said. 'So I challenge the AFL to set the record straight once and for all. If they have a problem with me staying on as president of the Carlton Football Club, let them come out and say so. If they don't have a problem, let them be unequivocal about it, then put the matter to rest.'[9]

Less than two months later the issue was resolved when the ACCC launched criminal proceedings against Pratt, claiming he had lied to its inquiry into the price-fixing allegations. As fate would have it, the morning Pratt was charged the Carlton board met in his Southbank offices. The mood was sombre and fearful as Pratt raged about the situation.

The following day, 20 June 2008, Richard Pratt stood down from the Carlton presidency. Gregg Swann said Stephen Kernahan, Pratt's deputy, would take over and painted Pratt's move as an expression of club loyalty, saying Pratt did not want his personal issues to distract the focus of the club. But the Blues were not letting go of their boss so easily. Three days later, Kernahan came out in support of Pratt, telling journalists that whatever happened he would support the Pratt family all the way.

Pratt stayed on as club patron, a position now taken by his wife Jeanne, and the club's home continues to be known as Visy Park following the signing of a three-year $1.5 million sponsorship deal. But Pratt was never afforded the chance to clear his name and return to Carlton, as ten months after he stepped down from his presidency prostate cancer took his life. Just one day before his death prosecutors dropped the charges against him after vital evidence in the case was ruled inadmissible.

Over the sixteen months Pratt dominated Carlton it is estimated he brought some $5 million to the club, a good part of it coming from his own pocket. The club's debt fell from $8 million to $6 million, despite embarking on the massive $30 million training centre project. The renaissance Pratt helped bring about has continued, with Carlton finishing eleventh on the ladder in 2008 with ten wins. Late in the 2009 season Carlton sat at fifth position on the AFL ladder.

On Sunday 21 June 2009, thousands of fans and Visy employees crowded into the stands at Carlton's Visy Park home to say goodbye and thank you to Richard Pratt. It was a farewell Pratt would have liked. Prime Minister Kevin Rudd gave a eulogy, while dignitaries sheltered from light rain under blue and white Visy umbrellas and Big John Elliott stood silent, puffing on his habitual cigarette. Pratt's daughter Heloise Waislitz carried on the family tradition of performance singing the Bette Midler number 'Wind Beneath My Wings' in memory of her father. All in all, it was a fitting way to see Richard Pratt out.

Chapter 10

Mr Fix-it

Richard Pratt was a natural communicator who believed
that to keep up in business you have to talk to your
suppliers, customers, employees, managers and those who are
making developments in the areas you are interested in. This
communication was also extended to his competitors, as he
thought it was important to maintain a culture of openness that
would enable him to remain alert to the nuance and culture
of the industries in which he worked. Discussions carried out
by Pratt and his executives with significant competitors often
ranged over issues such as the state of industrial relations, raw
material supplies and the possibility of the sale or purchase of
businesses from each other.

This philosophy eventually led Pratt into trouble. On
21 May 2001 Pratt lunched with Russell Jones, then the

managing director of Visy's number one competitor, Amcor, at the All Nations hotel in the inner-Melbourne suburb of Richmond. According to some accounts, over lunch the conversation between the two men strayed momentarily from the state of paper factories and glass supply and other industry chitchat to a price-fixing agreement. It was eventually agreed that at that lunch a commitment was made by Pratt to abide by an arrangement previously put in place and/or operated by executives including former Amcor Australasian chief Peter Brown and his subordinate Jim Hodgson and then Visy chief executive Harry Debney and another Visy executive Rod Carroll from 2000.

That arrangement had apparently not been adhered to by Visy, so Russell Jones was prevailed upon by Amcor Executives to ensure that Visy held up its end of the bargain. The deal was built on the understanding that the companies would not try to poach major customers from each other and would collaborate on the magnitude and timing of price rises.

Such tactics to divide the market between major producers have a long history in the cardboard packaging business. Before trade practices laws forbade such behaviour an association of box manufacturers would routinely list their main customers and the prices at which they were selling to them to ensure their competitors stayed away and pegged their own prices accordingly. Interestingly, Visy was said not to have been part of such arrangements, presumably because the company was growing at the time and interested in gaining market share, as opposed to simply holding on to what it already had. Or where it did enter the arrangements, it did not keep its side of the bargain, preferring instead to use it as a tool to win customers from competitors.

Until the late 1950s Australian Paper Mills (APM), the predecessor to Amcor, had a monopoly in the cardboard supply business. In order to hold on to this monopoly, APM gave discounts to customers in return for a commitment that they would buy all their materials from APM. These arrangements were eventually changed in response to pressure from its big customers when Smorgon Consolidated Industries entered the market. Such bold-faced arrangements were illegal by the 1970s but there were occasional breaches, including one in 2004 where Visy was fined $500 000 for trying to get a rival company to agree not to deal with Visy customers between 1996 and 1998.

In the early 2000s there was strong incentive for both Amcor and Visy to fix their prices. For fifteen years from the mid 1980s there had been intense competition in the cardboard packaging market as a result of Richard Pratt's ambitious expansion plans. Pratt had gone from a relatively insignificant box manufacturer when his father died in 1969, to a paper manufacturer with forty per cent market share of the cardboard packaging industry by the late 1980s, with the rest of the market split evenly between Smorgon and Amcor.

Smorgon was bought out by Pratt and Amcor in 1989 after a famous price war had all three competitors bleeding. Throughout the 1990s competition between Visy and Amcor remained fierce, keeping margins low, as big customers switched suppliers regularly. For this reason, the thought of market sharing would have held a strong attraction for both companies.

The cartel behaviour that emerged between Amcor and Visy in the early 2000s went beyond anything regulators had managed to unearth in the past and was a major coup for the Australian Competition and Consumer Commission (ACCC) chairman, Graeme Samuel. However, the ACCC did not uncover the miscreants itself. Information on the price-fixing arrangement emerged in another, altogether ironic, manner.

In August 2004 Amcor told executive Jim Hodgson that the company no longer required his services. Soon afterwards four other Amcor employees left the company, apparently deciding to consult to the packaging industry on their own account and forming a new venture called the Australasian Manufacturing Consulting Group.

Some of the former Amcor staffers had in their possession a lot of business information that Amcor considered was commercially sensitive. The company made legal moves to have the information returned. By November 2004 Amcor had achieved its wishes and the information was returned to its lawyers, Allens Arthur Robinson.

Allens perused the information and to its surprise noticed that it contained evidence that Amcor had been acting in ways that breeched competition laws. Most damaging was a series of tapes made between 2002 and 2004 by Hodgson of conversations between Hodgson, Visy's Harry Debney, Peter Sutton (then head of Amcor Australasia following the departure of Peter Brown who resigned in 2003 to start up a consultancy) and Brown discussing their cartel agreements. Some of the tapes contained talk about how the cartel arrangements split the market between the two groups, while others contained pretty colourful descriptions of their feelings and the characters involved in the arrangement.

'I am very nervous about [the cartel]', Debney says. Hodgson replies: 'Peter [Brown, then head of Amcor Australasia] is very very circumspect [about the cartel].'
Debney: 'Oh I know, so am I.'
Hodgson: 'You've got to be.'[1]

In another meeting Hodgson is told by his boss Sutton, 'Dick Pratt will wake up one morning and look at his growth figures over the past two years and say, "Shit, we haven't really grown much, that's no bloody good. Harry [Debney], get out there. I'm sick to death of this 'peace in our time' approach; fuck that, get out there and get me some business".'[2]

On one tape Sutton tells Hodgson that Pratt has 'a history of instability and irrational behaviour, and as he gets older there is no reason to believe he will get better'.[3] Some of the material was offensive. In one exchange Brown comments, 'Ah, you know what the Jews are like. No wonder they own half the world … I mean you'd reckon someone would go to the Palestinians and say, "Listen, you just can't beat this bunch. You're not fighting the Israelis, you're fighting the bloody Americans".'[4]

With this sort of material in their hands the lawyers felt they had no choice but to inform the Amcor board about the issues it raised. The board investigated and in December 2004 Russell Jones and his two subordinates resigned.

Until then Jones had been seen as a rising star of the Australian industrial scene after repairing damage done by some ill-starred offshore expansion and the price-cutting war of the late 1980s. He had boosted Amcor's profitability by hiving off the paper manufacturing business Paperlinx and developing major offshore packaging operations. Nonetheless, the cartel dealings meant a total fall from grace and he left the company with only minimum entitlements. Jones later admitted he had known about some price-fixing arrangements with Visy, but said that he had not realised their magnitude and was shocked by their comprehensive nature.

The cartel was not something Amcor's board could keep quiet about, so the board took the information to Graeme Samuel and the ACCC in late 2004. Under competition law, parties to anti-competitive behaviour can negotiate immunity from prosecution if they confess to the regulator and cease the behaviour. Within bounds in this case the first one to Graeme Samuel's door could get off without prosecution. Amcor took this option and immediately began negotiating total immunity from prosecution for the company and its executives. While the regulators granted a pardon the markets were not as forgiving.

Amcor's share price fell, major investors started asking questions about management and customers started talking about seeking compensation for the overcharging they had been subjected to while the cartel was operating. Some estimated that the industry had paid an extra $700 million over the four-year life of the cartel as a result of the price-fixing arrangement. Companies subjected to its effects included Ingham, Goodman Fielder, Nestlé Australia, Foster's, George Weston Foods, Merino, The Mildura Food Company, National Foods, Eagle Boys Dial-A-Pizza Australia, Gillette Australia, Parmalat Australia, the food and beverage division of Cadbury Schweppes and the Hardy Wine Company.[5]

Amcor obviously could not have a cartel by itself, so the ACCC began further investigations. Visy initially said it would investigate the situation, while Richard Pratt claimed that he knew nothing about it. Pratt continued with this line until the ACCC interviewed him in July 2005 when he admitted some knowledge. Meanwhile, Russell Jones admitted talking to Pratt about the cartel, even though Pratt continued to deny this was the case.

The ACCC investigation continued, clearly unconvinced by Pratt's earlier denials and explanations. On 21 December 2005 the ACCC launched proceedings against Visy, Richard Pratt, Harry Debney and Rod Carroll for price-fixing and market sharing in contravention of the Trade Practices Act, which the ACCC contended included dozens of secret meetings in venues such as parks and motels between staff of both companies over the four-year period.

For almost another two years the legal wheels creaked towards their conclusion. Then, on 8 October 2007, Pratt dropped a bombshell by signing an agreement with the ACCC in which he admitted to collusion with Amcor by himself and the company. In a brief statement he admitted that he had known about the cartel and that he had discussed it with Russell Jones during their lunch at the All Nations hotel. He attributed his about-face to having developed a better understanding of the situation following perusal of the ACCC's documents. The deal with the regulator meant that Visy and its officers did not have to face the formal trial scheduled for later that month.

Pratt told the media, 'The company deeply regrets what happened and its poor appreciation of the complexities and applications of the various provisions [of the Trade Practices Act]'. He said that his executives had 'erred' by holding secret talks with Amcor and that he accepted full responsibility for the comments he had made to Russell Jones over lunch, and that he apologised to all concerned.[6]

It was an embarrassing admission from a captain of industry, the president of an AFL football club and a leading philanthropist, and it led to the largest fine ever levied on a company for anti-competitive behaviour. On 1 November 2007 Federal Court judge Justice Peter Heerey levied a $36 million penalty against Visy, a $1.5 million fine to Harry Debney and a $500 000 fine to Rod Carroll. The courts did not levy a fine against Richard Pratt, considering the $36 million fine against Visy ultimately came from his pocket as owner. Visy's fine eclipsed the previous record, a $15 million fine against the Australian subsidiary of the Swiss group Roche.

While admitting the wrongdoing, Pratt claimed his customers had not suffered as a result of the price-fixing arrangement, with box prices falling not rising over the time of the cartel while Visy boosted its market share. The deal was aimed at wrong-footing Amcor, he said. Between 1998 and mid 2005 Visy's market share in the box industry rose from forty-six per cent to fifty-five per cent, while Amcor's fell from forty-seven per cent to thirty-six per cent. In a move that seemed designed to head off class actions by box users, Pratt said Visy would be happy to investigate any concerns its customers had about the situation.

Justice Heerey came down heavily on Visy's actions in his findings on the case, saying they were calculated and premeditated and that the case was 'by far the most serious cartel case to come before the court' in the thirty-plus years since cartel behaviour has been illegal in Australia. He continued, 'There cannot be any doubt that Mr Pratt also knew (along with Debney and Carroll) that the cartel, to which he gave his approval, and in which he has admitted to be knowingly concerned, was seriously unlawful.

'There is also the factor that the cartel was to operate for Mr Pratt's personal benefit, via his ownership, or part-ownership, of Visy. This was not a case of an employee acting out of some misguided sense of corporate loyalty.'[7]

In his decision Justice Heerey slammed Visy's corporate culture as non-existent in relation to its obligations under the Trade Practices Act, and said that Pratt, Carroll and Debney's regret seemed to stem from the fact that they were found out. 'None of the most senior people hesitated for a moment before embarking on obviously unlawful conduct', he said in his judgement.[8]

The judge did acknowledge that Pratt's involvement in the collusive behaviour was limited to the one meeting with Russell Jones at the All Nations hotel, but said this did not limit his complicity, as the behaviour could not have continued without his approval.

Pratt could do little more than take it on the chin. Despite his claim that customers had not suffered as a result of the price-fixing agreement it must still have been a major personal humiliation to change his story in that way, particularly after assuring then prime minister John Howard that he was innocent.

Harry Debney had fallen on his sword a month earlier, saying at the time that he was doing so to help take some of the spotlight off his old boss. As it turned out his action had no such effect and less than a year later he was almost a forgotten bit player in the drama.

On 19 June 2008 the ACCC launched criminal proceedings against Richard Pratt, accusing him of four counts of giving false and misleading information to an ACCC inquiry in

July 2005 when he claimed he had not discussed cartel arrangements with Russell Jones at the lunch in May 2001.

This really stirred things up. In the initial days following the breaking news of the cartel and in the years following there had been considerable discussion about the lack of teeth in Australia's anti-cartel legislation. In jurisdictions such as the US and some in Europe, criminal sanctions against corporate executives are quite common. That means those implementing illicit cartels can find themselves in jail, while in Australia, where the offences are civil, only fines can be levied, which in most cases are easily paid by the companies concerned. The Rudd Labor Government, elected in late 2007, pledged to introduce criminal sanctions in Australia, and in July 2009 an amendment to the Trade Practices Act was passed by parliament threatening jail terms of up to ten years for executives involved in flagrant and serious breaches.

In Visy's case a $36 million fine sounds like a lot of money, but with some commentators estimating that the cartel cost industry and consumers hundreds of millions in higher prices, the fine itself could be seen as a trifling cost of doing business. Until this stage it looked like the participants in the cartel had avoided anything other than monetary penalties, but the ACCC's stunning move against Richard Pratt meant that he could face as long as four years in jail if convicted.

The response to this move was loud and immediate, not least because of the unusual circumstances surrounding the laying of charges. Pratt and his family put out a statement saying they were shocked by the new charges and that they would be vigorously defended. Pratt himself pledged that he would stand down from all public positions until the situation was resolved. This meant resigning as president of his beloved

Carlton Football Club, a position he had held for only fourteen months, and ceasing his official involvement with the family's philanthropic arm, The Pratt Foundation. Some high-profile people came out in his defence, while Pratt's lawyer, Leon Zwier, labelled the move an abuse of process.

What irked the Pratt camp and shocked some in the business and legal communities was the fact that in their eyes the issue had been put to bed back in October 2007 when an agreement was reached with the ACCC to settle the civil case. However, in July 2005 when Richard Pratt was interviewed by the ACCC regarding the cartel, Pratt claimed there had been no discussion of anything to do with the cartel at his May 2001 lunch with Russell Jones, and that Jones was lying in claiming there was. But in the agreed statement of facts resulting from mediations with the ACCC in the run-up to their October 2007 agreements, Pratt made admissions to the contrary.

The ACCC now felt that Pratt had a case to answer for what was effectively perjury—lying to an ACCC investigation. What incensed the Pratt camp was their view that they had been deceived when making the October 2007 agreement. The chairman of a September 2007 mediation session that led to agreement and the production of the Agreed Statement of Facts in October, former High Court judge Michael McHugh, said that the ACCC had never let on that there was any possibility of prosecuting Pratt on the basis of the statements he made in July 2005. 'Had the ACCC informed me of such risks or possibilities, I would have regarded that as a relevant matter to put to Mr Pratt in considering whether to compromise the civil penalty proceeding', McHugh said in a statement read to the Federal Court in December 2008.[9]

The Pratt camp stated that the statement of agreed facts signed in October 2007 was made merely to effect settlement of the case. Michael McHugh said that even during the mediation, with the ACCC in one room and Pratt and his lawyers in another, the businessman had again denied discussing the cartel with Jones. McHugh also told the ACCC that if the case were to go to trial it would come down to one man's word against another's and that it would be up to the ACCC to prove the veracity of Jones's claims.

In his testimony to the ACCC Jones had said that when the topic of not poaching each others customers came up at the lunch Pratt clearly understood the content of the discussion and confirmed that the arrangement would be adhered to by Visy.[10]

The ACCC backed up its position by saying that it was applying the law without fear or favour, but in the media and the business community a view was emerging that this was some sort of personal clash between two titans, Dick Pratt and ACCC Chairman Graeme Samuel. Both were high-profile and respected figures in the business community, the Jewish community and the world of AFL football. Samuel is a former Macquarie Bank director and served as AFL commissioner. The two had been friends in the past, with Samuel having been on occasion a guest at Raheen for the well-known Sunday meals, but they reportedly fell out sometime in the mid 1990s.

John Elliott, former Carlton president and, in his days as head of the Foster's brewing empire, a one-time major Visy customer, came out in defence of Pratt. On radio he described Pratt as one of the country's most generous men. 'This thing looks very much like the tall-poppy syndrome and looks like a very vindictive act in my view', Elliott said.[11]

Graeme Samuel moved quickly to counter such views and their implied slur to his professional reputation. On 27 June 2008 he told the National Press Club that while there had been much talk of decisions being made for personal motives, all decisions made by the ACCC are made by all seven commissioners and that almost every decision made over the previous five years had been unanimous.

Samuel said that all ACCC decisions were made after 'careful consideration and rigorous analysis'. He added that the ACCC's decision-making process was subject to 'scrutiny and review by the courts', and that the organisation's powers were bound by 'the principles of administrative law, which include tests of natural justice, reasonableness, proper purpose and good faith'.[12]

By this time in the proceedings another ingredient had made its way into the Shakespearian-like drama—Richard Pratt's prostate cancer had returned. First diagnosed in 2006, it appeared not to stem the industrialist's renowned energy and restlessness. By late 2007 the disease was in remission, but Michael McHugh reported that Richard Pratt did not seem to be in good health throughout the mediations leading up to the settlement.

By 2009 Pratt's criminal prosecution and his cancer were drawing to their conclusions. Journalist Cameron Stewart, who had built up a relationship with Pratt, wrote a long assessment of the man in *The Australian* and included material published around the time of the ACCC settlement in 2007. At the time Pratt obviously felt the need to explain himself and talk publicly about how the legal battle and his admission of involvement in the cartel was affecting him. He described how he wrestled with his decision to go 'to court to explain myself and try to clear my name or [seek] a negotiated settlement, which will necessarily involve admissions of breaking the law. On balance, the appropriate thing to do is settle [with the ACCC]'.[13]

The damage caused to Pratt's reputation by the price-fixing scandal and his resulting fall from grace clearly weighed heavily on him in his final days. He spoke of his anger to Stewart, saying, 'My reputation is something I have been building for fifty years and so I am worried that the general public will now see me as a rich person who has made his money doing something that is wrong in the eyes of the law'.[14]

As April wore on Pratt's illness worsened and his family announced that he was close to death. But Pratt did not want to leave this world without getting his temporal affairs in order, so he kicked his legal team into action once more. They were to attempt to get key evidence in the criminal case (the agreed statement of facts made with the ACCC in 2007 to facilitate settlement of the cartel case) tossed out of court.

On Friday 24 April Pratt's lawyer, Leon Zwier, asked Justice Donnell Ryan to make an immediate ruling under what is known as an 'indulgence' on the permissibility of the ACCC's use of the statement of facts as evidence. Zwier gave Justice Ryan a brief on Pratt's medical condition, but emphasised that he was not asking for the criminal proceedings to be abandoned because of ill health. He wanted to leave the proceedings in place hoping the ACCC case would collapse if the judge disallowed the ACCC's evidence. Richard Pratt was trying to clear his name on his death bed.

The judge refused to act on the spot but said he would examine the matter over the weekend. On the following Monday 27 April, Justice Ryan ruled that the agreed statement of fact could not be used as evidence against Pratt. The Commonwealth Director of Public Prosecutions (DPP) immediately dropped its case against the dying industrialist, a move many saw as vindicating Pratt. 'He'll at least pass into the next world knowing that he has been vindicated, and he is innocent', close friend and well-known Melbourne lawyer Mark Leibler said outside court.[15]

A day later, on 28 April 2009, Richard Pratt passed away. However, Pratt's dying wish for vindication was not fully granted. Though he went to his grave without criminal action pending against him, the DPP, in what some saw as a face-saving exercise, said it had dropped the case because of Pratt's poor health. The DPP would not run a case that had no chance of success and with Pratt expected to die any day there was no chance of a successful prosecution being obtained.

The ACCC put out a press release the day after Pratt's death saying it had other evidence on which to build a case against Pratt and it had not considered the material ruled on by Justice Ryan as admissible until late in the development of the case. 'The prosecution's case filed in this matter would have relied upon a range of evidence, most of which was not the subject of Justice Ryan's orders on 27 April 2009. The ACCC and its officers, in their investigation and decision making processes, have acted at all times properly and in good faith in pursuit of their public responsibilities', the press release read.[16]

∽✤∽

Undoubtedly Richard Pratt will go down in the history of the cardboard packaging industry as in a league of his own. After starting out in the late 1960s with one box factory, Visy now has fifty-five per cent market share, compared with thirty-six per cent for Amcor, the public company that was once a monopoly supplier. Although nearly pushed into oblivion during the 'box wars' of the late 1980s, Pratt stood his ground and was one of only two survivors after the Smorgon company left the industry. Pratt also successfully moved into the American market and the $5 million company he began with is now worth around $3.5 billion.

Was Pratt guilty of running a cartel for four years in the early 2000s? Yes, by his own admission he was. He said his customers did not suffer as a result of it and that he only used the arrangements as a means of giving himself a competitive advantage over Amcor, presumably by preventing them from bidding for his customers. These claims will be tested in late 2009 and in 2010 when thousands of Visy and Amcor customers bring class actions against both companies to try to win over $300 million in compensation for what they say is the over-charging they endured because of the cartel.

An interesting side story in the cartel affair was the matter of Richard Pratt's Order of Australia medals. Pratt received the Officer of the Order of Australia in 1985 for services to industry, the arts and sport, and in 1998 it was upgraded to Companion of the Order of Australia, the highest award in the country. In an embarrassing move, in February 2008 Pratt handed the awards back, apparently after learning that the Council for the Order of Australia was in the process of deciding whether to strip him of them.

There were some precedents for this action. Businessman Rodney Adler handed back his award following his conviction and jailing over his role at the HIH insurance group, which collapsed in 2001. His fellow HIH director Ray Williams was stripped of his award after he also was convicted and jailed over the affair, while former judge Marcus Einfeld lost his award after being jailed for perjury and attempting to pervert the course of justice.

While these men were convicted on criminal charges Pratt handed back his award before any criminal charges could be laid against him, and before new rules came in barring those convicted on civil charges from receiving awards. Television funny man and entertainment entrepreneur Steve Vizard received an Order of Australia in 1997 and held onto it after being found to have misused his position as a Telstra director to trade in shares in three companies. However, in May 2008 Vizard handed back his award after the ban on awards for those convicted of civil offences was introduced.

Richard Pratt paid a high price for his involvement in the cardboard cartel with Amcor. While criminal charges against him were dropped on his deathbed, he chose to give up important public roles in a number of areas following his 2007 admission of wrongdoing, and he had to wear a good deal of public opprobrium. It would have been a difficult burden to bear towards the end of what was in many ways a very successful life and career.

Chapter 11

The Legacy of a Cardboard King

Just as Richard Pratt lived a huge life, he also leaves behind a massive legacy. The Pratts are now Australia's richest family, with an estimated net worth of $4.3 billion, despite the global financial crisis that struck late in 2007. Anthony Pratt has taken up the mantle that has beckoned to him most of his life—that is, the mantle of leading Visy as Chairman in ways that are appropriate for him, rather than for his father. The Pratt family is in transition, just as it was following the death of Leon Pratt in 1969. Back then even Richard's leadership skills were doubted, but he proved the sceptics so wrong it is now laughable. Similarly, there are also those who doubt whether Anthony can replicate his father's success.

Family transition can often be problematic, but Anthony Pratt has already proven he is ready for his new position at the head of Visy by increasing the profits of Visy's US operation from US$100 million to US$1 billion in fifteen years. Visy's recycling ethos, which started as a means for the then small company to succeed in the market against big competitors, has now become an asset in itself, and in 2007 Anthony committed Pratt Industries USA to investing US$1 billion in projects aimed at dealing with climate change as part of a global initiative launched by former president Bill Clinton. Many of the investment projects, which include recycling operations and waste-to-energy plants, were on the company agenda anyway, Anthony admits, but signing up to the Clinton initiative helps put the desirability and viability of such projects up in lights. One such highly visible project, a US$50 million waste-to-energy gasifier at Visy's paper mill in Georgia, will be completed by the time this book goes to print, producing nine megawatts of electricity and cutting carbon dioxide emissions by 75 000 tonnes a year. Visy's recycling operations in the US yield greenhouse emission reductions equivalent to taking 360 000 cars off the road, and the recycling of aluminium cans uses ninety-five per cent less electricity than making new ones.

Anthony is different from his father, more methodical and systematic, and more inclined to call for a feasibility study on projects before acting. This suggests he will be a more cautious leader than his father, who would take big leaps involving calculated risks when he thought it necessary. However, he has already taken a step forward in cementing his position as leader. On 19 August 2009 the Pratt family announced that Visy chief executive John Murphy had resigned and that Anthony would move from joint-chair to executive chairman. A former Visy division chief, Chris Daly, was appointed Chief Operating Officer of the group. It was a significant move; Anthony has increased his power at Visy in order to have greater influence on the day-to-day operations and direction. He has taken back the operational control that Richard handed to Murphy and his predecessor Harry Debney from 2000.

Murphy, appointed following Debney's resignation in September 2007, was an important hiring for Visy. He came from a public company background at Foster's Beverage Group and implemented a tighter corporate governance regime Richard deemed necessary after the cartel scandal. But at times he had difficulty dealing with Visy's private company culture. Visy says Murphy's governance measures will stay in place, but Anthony has also signalled that he will take a strong global leadership role in the group and is not prepared to leave such authority with managers. He plans to make his mark on the business and it will be interesting to see what mark that is.

Analysts watching Visy say the company is performing better than rival Amcor in the Australian packaging space, delivering returns to its owners of between fifteen per cent and eighteen per cent compared with about nine per cent for its competitor. Visy would be an attractive proposition for a float on the stock market or a trade sale to another company. There has been speculation for years that New Zealand forests products group Carter Holt Harvey, owned by Australasia's richest man Graeme Hart, is a potential suitor. While Richard was alive the prospect of a sale or partial float was considered low as he was fiercely independent and had had bad experiences on public markets. However, with a new generation in control such possibilities may be considered if the Pratt family sees them as being in their best interests.

While Richard Pratt may have wanted to keep Visy a private family concern, he wisely began succession planning some years ago. As a result, each of his and Jeanne's three children and their families have their own operations outside the Visy banner. Heloise and Alex Waislitz own the Thorney investment group, Fiona and Raphael Geminder the Pact packaging operation, and Anthony and Claudine Pratt have Pratt Industries, Visy's US offshoot. This leaves each of the children with their own interests, as well as a jointly held stake in Visy, giving them both independence and a family connection. Presumably Pratt also intended that each have an established career path if Visy were sold off down the track.

Anthony has already had to deal with some difficult issues left over from his father's rule. Visy has settled a court case with confectionary group Cadbury, which was seeking recompense for what it saw as financial damage caused to it by the Visy–Amcor cardboard cartel. No settlement figure was ever released to the public. Visy also faces a class action from hundreds of other cardboard box users also seeking recompense for alleged damage caused by the price-fixing arrangement. It is not clear when this matter will be resolved.

There is much more to Richard Pratt's legacy than simply his business achievements, as remarkable as these may have been. The boundless energy, insight, money and ideas he invested in a wide range of interests meant that when he had gone an enormous array of people felt the need to express their sorrow and gratitude. Prime Minister Kevin Rudd, Victorian Premier John Brumby, actress Rachel Griffiths and World

Vision Chief Executive Tim Costello were among those to publicly praise Pratt's contribution to society in the days following his death.

But there were detractors as well. Former independent federal MP and football personality Phil Cleary called Mr Brumby to task, saying that while he respected the grief of the Pratt family, people should not forget that Visy had been involved in price-fixing, and that it was sad to see the Premier ignoring that. 'Richard Pratt and his company robbed many ordinary Australians, according to a finding made in the courts, and the Premier just glosses over it', Mr Cleary said at the time. 'Why are they all so full of praise for Richard Pratt? It's because many of them are recipients of his philanthropy.'[1]

Nevertheless, the state of Victoria offered the Pratt family a state memorial service for Richard, which was held on 21 June 2009 in the Victorian Arts Centre's Hamer Hall. Speakers at the service reflected on the wide range of areas Pratt had traversed over the course of his life. A tribute was given by Premier Brumby, who described Richard as 'a force of nature', and 'one of those rare people who has the ability to make possible what was previously only imagined'. He was followed by Winsome McCaughey, former executive director of Australian Business Arts Foundation and former Melbourne Lord Mayor, who said Richard 'valued the arts and education for their transformative force'. BHP Billiton Chairman Don Argus paid tribute to his business legacy, while AFL Chief Executive Andrew Demetriou spoke of Pratt's contribution to Australian football. Australian Conservation Foundation Chief Don Henry described Visy as 'at its core an environmental company', and said Pratt had been a catalyst in developing the sort of actions being taken in water conservation today. Anthony Pratt finished up the service and the bandwagon rolled on to Visy Park for a 'family day' to celebrate Pratt's life.

A month later, on Friday 24 July 2009, the Carlton Football Club took the field to play the inaugural Richard Pratt Cup match against the Collingwood Football Club. Carlton coach Brett Ratten commented that the cup would be a tribute to the man who had greatly influenced the club and the game in general. The match was also used to raise awareness of prostate cancer, which had claimed Pratt's life. Unfortunately for the club, Collingwood trounced Carlton, winning ninety-four points to forty points.

Richard Pratt and the motivations that drove him are hard to sum up in a few words. He goes down in history as one of Australia's greatest businessmen. Not simply because he built a huge international empire from a relatively modest beginning; Rupert Murdoch outshone him in that department. Not just because in his dying moments he became Australia's richest person; a number of people have held that epithet over the decades, albeit some more forgettable than others. Not just because he was hugely generous; others like the Potter, Lowy and Myer families have also given much to society over a long period. Not because he was outspoken; so too have been business leaders such as Hugh Morgan and Lang Hancock.

What made Richard Pratt unique was the fact that on top of his success he had passions and interests that ranged across a wide range of areas, and he also had the energy and enthusiasm to personally engage with them. Few business leaders have the capacity to pursue their own careers and be actively involved in philanthropy, the arts and sporting activities the way Richard was. Many sign cheques, but few actually come to the meetings or drive change in the organisations.

While some successful businesspeople are outspoken, usually it is in areas that pertain to their businesses, which can appear as narrow self-interest. Those employing large, low-paid workforces often want to weaken the power of organised labour, those with uranium mines frequently desire nuclear energy, and most people in business want lower taxes and less government intervention. There is nothing wrong with wanting these things. Richard Pratt wanted some of these things, too.

But Richard's outspokenness had a visionary quality to it that was reinforced by a desire to act. His calls for water reform were backed up by investment in research into water usage. Had his plans to pipe irrigation channels gone ahead, no doubt he would have invested the necessary millions to allow Visy to supply recycled plastic pipes for the project. Yes, that would have made him money, but the whole project had an inspirational quality to it that helped the nation focus on the need to think about and deal with water differently.

Richard Pratt, to use his own terminology, 'put his body in'. He lived life with a sort of exuberance that inspired others. Not only did he provide entertainment for customers and staff, he got up and sang himself. Not only did he give money to the arts, he rolled up his sleeves and got involved in helping to deliver the arts better. Not only did he call for environmental awareness, he spent $1 billion on a state-of-the-art environmental pulp mill, fighting all the necessary battles along the way. When he had a child outside his marriage he did not leave her on the sidelines, but took an active part in her life and made her a part of his wider family.

Richard Pratt could be engaging and good company. He could also be withdrawn, morose and downright difficult. As Sam Lipski observed at his funeral, 'He was loved because of who he was, and despite the way he sometimes was. A great man, and yet everyman. A great Australian, wealthy and powerful, and yet every Australian. He was profoundly human, yet writ large'.[2] Pratt confronted things head on. When caught out price-fixing he set out to clean up his corporate game and appointed former ACCC chairman Professor Allan Fels to Visy's compliance committee.

It is difficult to guess what part the price-fixing scandal will play in the Richard Pratt story in the long term. He, by his own admission, took part in illegal cartel behaviour, and he paid the penalty both in terms of his reputation and with Australia's largest fine for such an offence. Criminal charges for lying to the ACCC inquiry examining the cartel case were dropped the day before his death after a judge ruled a major piece of the ACCC supporting evidence as inadmissible. Regulators said they had other evidence they could use, but that Pratt's imminent death prevented them from doing so. Pratt's supporters said he was exonerated, and he died without the odium of criminality surrounding him.

Richard Pratt was also Australia's most generous philanthropist, giving away at least $150 million over the course of his life. Did he do it to boost his influence? That may have been one of his motivations. But he also held that generosity was an important quality and that it gave him the means to bolster the organisations and causes he believed in. Does his generosity cancel out his wrongdoing? Pratt's Jewish religion holds that a man's good deeds sit alongside his transgressions, neither diminishing nor cancelling the other, with only God entitled to weigh the balance.

After Pratt's death there was a call from supporters to reinstate his Companion of the Order of Australia award, handed back voluntarily during the controversy over the price-fixing agreement. Seeing as the Council for the Order of Australia has since ruled that those guilty of civil offences cannot receive the honour it is unlikely this will happen.

Meanwhile, Jeanne Pratt retains her Companion of the Order of Australia and seems intent on continuing to carry the family banner in the arts and philanthropy. In July 2009 she launched the new season of her theatre group, The Production Company, with the show *Crazy for You*. The opening night was dedicated to Richard. She is set to retain Raheen as a cultural and philanthropic centre for Melbourne, as well as a place to fly the Visy flag. She has taken up the role as patron of Carlton Football Club, picking up the mantle of one of her husband's greatest passions. And she is co-chair of Visy with Anthony, so her influence in the business will remain strong.

Richard Pratt led a remarkable and colourful life. He created wealth for himself and his family, jobs for thousands, commercialised recycling and boosted the green economy. He supported the arts and culture, he stood on toes, he inspired, he entertained, he frustrated and he intimidated. He celebrated his success, sharing it with the world through philanthropy, he had fun, he sinned, he flaunted convention and he implemented new dreams. And, strangely for a man so committed to private business, he did most of this in the public eye. He will be, as they say in show business, a hard act to follow.

Notes

Chapter 1

1   G Linnell, 'The secrets of his success', *Good Weekend*, 2 December 2000.

2   Linnell.

3   S Lipski, *The Pratt Story*, Conlay Press, 1984.

4   Y Segelman, *Take Action!* Lothian Books, Melbourne, 2004.

5   Linnell.

6   Linnell.

7   *Herald Sun*, 27 April 1995.

8   C Stewart, 'Richard Pratt, the great enabler', *The Australian*, 29 April 2009.

9   Lipski.

Chapter 2

1   Lipski.

2   R Myer, *Living the Dream: The Story of Victor Smorgon*, New Holland, 2000.

3   Lipski.

4   Lipski.

5   Lipski.

6   Lipski.

7   K Maley, 'Pratt prepared to deal with the devil for sale', *The Sydney Morning Herald*, 16 August 1991.

8   R Myer, 'The scam that fooled Melbourne', *The Sunday Age*, 1 October 1995.

9   'Pratt not going broke', *The Herald*, 9 April 1990.

10   A Shand, 'Packaging the legacy', *The Australian Financial Review*, 15 December 2000.

11   Shand.

Chapter 3

1   J Stensholt, 'The rich get poorer', *BRW*, 28 May 2009, p. 83.

2   Stensholt.

3   *Herald Sun*, 6 October 2003.

4   T Gray & S Webster, *You Don't Know What You Don't Know 'Til You Know It*, Information Australia, Melbourne, 2000.

5   Gray & Webster.

6   R Gottliebsen, 'Pratt family's succession lessons', *BRW*, 10 March 1997.

7   *Family Business*, June 1997.

Chapter 4

1   *BRW*, 8 September 1997.

2   Speech to the Family Business Council, 16 October 1997.

3   Gray & Webster.

4   Address to the Melbourne Rotary Club, 17 March 1995.

5   Gray & Webster.

6   *The Age*, 15 June 1998.

7   *The Age*, 15 June 1998.

8   Gray & Webster.

9   Gray & Webster.

Chapter 5

1   B Roberts, *Raheen: A House and its People*, Pola Nominees, 2007.

2   *Herald Sun*, 17 March 1999.

3   *The Age*, 17 March 1999.

4   *Australian Financial Review*, 21 September 1998.

5   Gray & Webster.

6   *Herald Sun*, 17 July 2000.

Chapter 6

1   *Australian Jewish News*, 11 October 1998.

2   Philanthropy Australia fact sheet, 'Australia's 10 largest reporting foundations', Philanthropy Australia, 18 May 2009.

3   *The Australian Financial Review*, 15 February 2000.

4   *The Age*, 27 June 1998.

5   R Brunton, *Richard Pratt, Cultural Entrepreneur*, Pola Nominees, Melbourne, 2004.

6   Brunton.

7   Brunton.

8   Linnell.

9   C Stewart, 'Richard Pratt profile: a rich man's world', *Weekend Australian Magazine*, 6 October 2007.

10   Brunton.

11   Linnell.

Chapter 7

1   B Hills, 'The billionaire, his lover, their nanny and her hush money', *The Sydney Morning Herald*, 15 March 2000.

2   'Pratt—the story behind the story', *Media Watch*, ABC TV, 27 March 2000.

3   A Sharp, 'Inside the world of a kept woman, Shari-Lea Hitchcock', *The Daily Telegraph*, 1 May 2009.

4   S Gare, 'Money as a mistress is a bit rich', *The Australian*, 18 March 2000.

5   B Mitchell, 'Pratt drops another ball', *The Australian*, 12 May 2000.

6   Stewart.

7   Stewart.

8   Sharp.

9   A Hornery, 'I'm being judged but I'm putting my daughter first', *The Sydney Morning Herald*, 9 May 2009.

10 Stewart, 'Richard Pratt profile: a rich man's world'.

Chapter 8

1   A West & F Walker, 'Pratt's $100m offer to water the outback', *The Sydney Morning Herald*, 15 September 2002.

2   'Richard Pratt warns of coming chronic shortage of water', The World Today Archive, ABC Radio, 14 March 2003.

3   Visy/ANZ press release, 'Pratt, ANZ link to provide water saving loans', 3 February 2004.

4   *The Australian*, 25 November 1999.

5   T Stephens, 'Debt is good for you, tycoon tells MPs', *The Sydney Morning Herald*, 20 January 2005.

6   Stephens.

7   *The Age*, 18 June 1998.

Chapter 9

1   Linnell.

2   Linnell.

3   A Hawkins & G McLauchlan, *The Hawk*, Four Star Books, Auckland, 1989.

4   P Smith, 'Carlton salary fine adds to Elliott embarrassment', *The Australian*, 13 October 2000.

5   Smith.

6   C Le Grand, 'Elliott leaves legacy of doubt', *The Australian*, 12 November 2002.

7   Staff writers, 'Former Carlton president Richard Pratt dies after long battle with cancer,' Fox Sports, 28 April 2009.

8   G Denham, 'Blues become Judd's chosen ones', *The Australian*, 3 October 2007.

9   R Pratt, 'President's address', President's function: Carlton versus Collingwood, 13 April 2008.

Chapter 10

1   C Stewart & B Speedy, 'Sounds of collusion caught on tape', *The Australian*, 10 December 2007.

2   Stewart & Speedy.

3   Stewart & Speedy.

4   N Levin & D Levin, 'Amcor anti-Semitic slurs anger community leaders', *Australian Jewish News*, 15 October 2007.

5   L Gettler, 'Visy cartel case puts price fixers on notice', *The Age*, 17 October 2007.

6   L Wood, 'Pratt: the confessions of a multi-billionaire', *The Age*, 9 October 2007.

7   L Wood, 'Pratt's cartel "cost all of us"', *The Age*, 9 October 2007.

8   L Wood, 'Pratt's cartel "cost all of us"'.

9   L Wood, 'Watchdog feels weight of Pratt's fall', *The Age*, 13 December 2008.

10 L Wood, 'Shades of grey', *The Age*, 15 September 2008.

11 L Wood, 'Loyal friend's blustering testimonial no help to Pratt', *The Age*, 21 June 2008.

12 A Browne, 'Pratt proceedings "not personal"', *Australian Jewish News*, 26 June 2008.

13 Stewart, 'Richard Pratt, the great enabler'.

14 Stewart, 'Richard Pratt, the great enabler'.

15 A Sharp & M Dobbin, 'Pratt wins the last round over ACCC', *The Age*, 28 April 2009.

16 ACCC press release NR 095/09, 29 April 2009.

Chapter 11

1   L Wood, A Sharp & P Millar, 'ACCC unbowed as mourners gather', *The Age*, 30 April 2009.

2   S Lipski, 'History will smile on a man of honour', *The Australian*, 1 May 2009.

Index